INTERMEDIATE 2 and HIGHER
Physical Education
course notes – **2nd edition**

✕ Malcolm Thorburn ✕

Intermediate 2 & Higher Physical Education

Contents

Welcome

Intermediate 2 and Higher Level Physical Education is about **your** practical experience of Physical Education. Your participation is active and demanding: you work and learn with your class colleagues and teachers in a challenging and rewarding environment.

These *Course Notes and Questions and Answers* are designed to help you understand relevant concepts involved in Physical Education at Intermediate 2 and Higher Level.

Physical Education at these levels is useful:

- ○ **for your own interest and self-development**
- ○ **as a subject to add breadth and balance to your other subjects**
- ○ **as part of a Group Award in Sport and Leisure**
- ○ **as part of your entry requirements for Further and Higher Education, especially if you want to study Physical Education at a more advanced level, perhaps with a view to following a career in sport and related industries**

Unit/Course Outline and Assessment

Higher Still qualifications are made up of **Units** and **Course awards**.

Two Units make up a Course award at Intermediate 2 and Higher Level. These are:

- Performance Unit

- Analysis and Development of Performance Unit

Performance Unit

You agree the activities for your Unit and Course with your teacher and class colleagues. The activities you agree will reflect the interests of the whole group and take into account practical considerations, such as available facilities. As you develop your skills as a performer your teacher will give you feedback on how well you are improving. You can also use your free time to develop your ability. Try to set realistic improvement targets.

You are assessed by your teacher in the different activities. He or she will give you details about your level of performance and tell you when it is at the required level to achieve the Unit. If you achieve the Performance Unit, you can use it as part of your Course award in Physical Education.

You can achieve a Unit at a level above that in which you are completing a Course award. This allows you to gain credit for your achievement. It may be, for example, that you could get credit for having achieved a Course award overall at Intermediate 2, whilst gaining extra Unit credit for having achieved the Unit in Performance at Higher Level.

Analysis and Development of Performance Unit

The four areas of **Analysis and Development of Performance** are:

- **Area 1** **Performance Appreciation**
- **Area 2** **Preparation of the Body**
- **Area 3** **Skills and Techniques**
- **Area 4** **Structures, Strategies and Composition**

Your Analysis and Development of Performance will include the study of at least three of these areas. Each of these areas of Analysis and Development and Performance is made up of a number of **Key Concepts**. These are briefly outlined on page 6 and form the basis of pages 8 to 93.

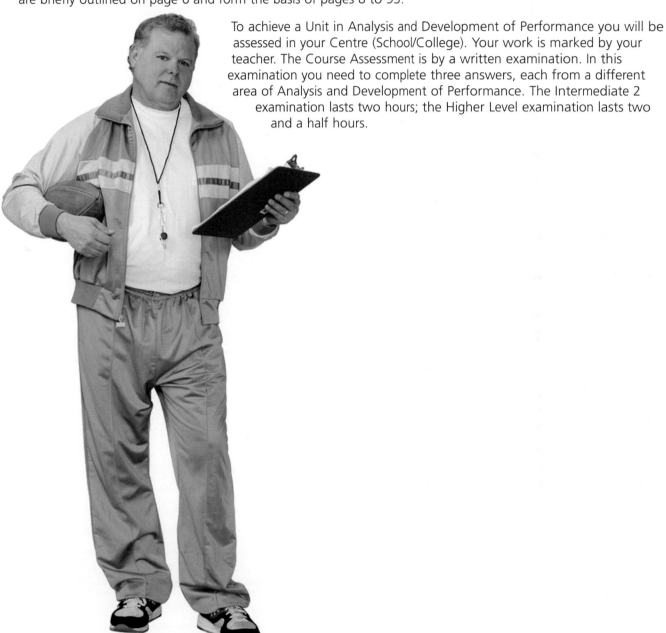

To achieve a Unit in Analysis and Development of Performance you will be assessed in your Centre (School/College). Your work is marked by your teacher. The Course Assessment is by a written examination. In this examination you need to complete three answers, each from a different area of Analysis and Development of Performance. The Intermediate 2 examination lasts two hours; the Higher Level examination lasts two and a half hours.

1 INTRODUCTION

Performance Appreciation (Area 1)

is a **general** broad view of performance which relates to the three other specific areas of Analysis of Performance. The **Key Concepts** in this area are:

- Overall nature and demands of quality performance
- Technical, physical, personal and special qualities of performance
- Mental factors influencing performance
- Use of appropriate models of performance
- Planning and managing personal performance improvement

Preparation of the Body (Area 2)

is a **specific** analysis of the fitness and training requirements necessary for your performance. The **Key Concepts** in this area are:

- Fitness assessment in relation to personal performance and the demands of activities
- Application of different types of fitness in the development of activity specific performance
- Physical, skill-related and mental aspects of fitness.
- Principles and methods of training
- Planning, implementing and monitoring training

Skills and Techniques (Area 3)

is a **specific** analysis of your skills and techniques needs in performance. The **Key Concepts** in this area are:

- The concept of skill and skilled performance
- Skill/technique improvement through mechanical analysis or movement analysis or consideration of quality
- The development of skill and the refinement of technique

Structures, Strategies and Composition (Area 4)

is a **specific** analysis of the influence of shape, form and design on your performance. The **Key Concepts** in this area are:

- The structures, strategies and/or compositional elements that are fundamental to activities
- Identification of strengths and weaknesses in performance in terms of:
  - roles and relationships, formations, tactical or design elements, choreography and composition
- Information processing, problem-solving and decision-making when working to develop and improve performance

Assessment

To achieve a Unit you have to complete successfully the Unit Assessments. To achieve the Course award, i.e. Physical Education at Intermediate 2 or Higher Level, you have to complete successfully the Unit Assessments and the Course award Assessments at the chosen level of presentation.

Course Award Aggregation

When you complete all the Course Assessments a final mark will be calculated. This final mark is based on the following weighting:

- ● **Performance counts as 40% of your final mark at Higher Level, 50% at Intermediate 2 Level.**
- ● **Analysis and Development of Performance counts as 60% of your final mark at Higher Level, 50% at Intermediate 2 Level.**

You can achieve a Course award with an 'A', 'B' or 'C' pass depending on your final mark.

What other resources you have

In addition to these *Course Notes and Questions and Answers* and your own class notes there are a wide variety of textbooks, videos and sport-related websites that you may find useful. When checking the usefulness of books, videos and websites identify those, which benefit your Performance and the different areas of Analysis and Development of Performance. Use your school library and local library to locate resources. Relevant books have many uses. You may find some chapters useful in order to expand on issues raised in these *Course Notes and Questions and Answers*. They may also help your preparation for the Analysis and Development of Performance Course examination. There are many books and videos on the market, but only some of them relate directly to the Intermediate 2 and Higher Level work. Check carefully before choosing.

What these notes cover

These *Course Notes and Questions and Answers* are divided into seven sections: the first five sections provide you with valuable Analysis and Development of Performance information which helps you understand how the different Analysis and Development of Performance areas and Key Concepts relate to your Performance study. These sections also contain revision questions to help you check on your learning progress. The sixth section provides you with advice about how to prepare for your Unit and Course Assessments. The seventh section provides Unit and Course Assessment examples at both Intermediate 2 and Higher Level. An answer pull out section with exemplar answers to the questions about the different Key Concepts in the Analysis and Development of Performance is also included.

 Write down how your activities link to the different areas of Analysis and Development of Performance.

2 BEGINNING YOUR ANALYSIS AND DEVELOPMENT OF PERFORMANCE

The design model for Analysis and Development of Performance

Analysis and Development of Performance has these four areas:

- Area 1   **Performance Appreciation**
- Area 2   **Preparation of the Body**
- Area 3   **Skills and Techniques**
- Area 4   **Structures, Strategies and Composition**

The diagram below shows how the four areas relate to each other. *Performance Appreciation* takes a general overview of Performance and all that it includes. The other three areas look at specific areas of performance.

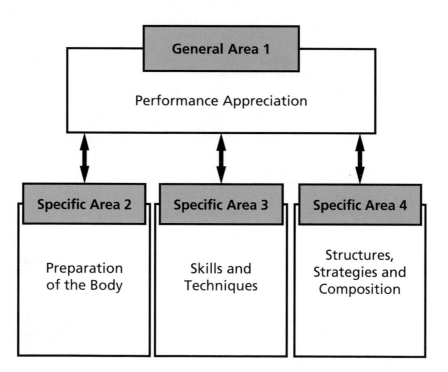

Note how the two-way arrows in the diagram link *Performance Appreciation* to the three other areas. Each area includes a number of **Key Concepts**. When you are studying Key Concepts within Performance Appreciation, consider how they relate to specific Key Concepts in the other three areas. Likewise, when studying Area 2, 3 or 4, relate your work in that area to Key Concepts in Area 1.

Understanding this link between areas is essential at the outset of your Analysis and Development of Performance work. Do not, however, link together Key Concepts from across the three specific areas.

The key point to remember is that your Analysis and Development of Performance work will involve you in linking your understanding from the *general* to the *specific* and from the *specific* to the *general*.

Your teacher will explain to you, which performance activities relate to the different areas of Analysis and Development of Performance. Understanding this relationship is very important. If you are unsure, **ask!**

An Integrated Approach

Consider this example. In working practically at basketball, your Analysis and Development of Performance could cover some aspects of **Performance Appreciation** in general and **Preparation of the Body** in specific detail.

In **Performance Appreciation** your Analysis of Performance could cover the **Key Concepts** of 'the overall nature and demands of quality performance' and the 'mental factors influencing performance'. So, your Analysis and Development of Performance could include:

- nature of basketball, e.g. team, set rules, expected codes of conduct (nature/demands)
- performance demands, e.g. different roles, working to your potential (nature/demands)
- managing your emotions during demanding performance (mental factors)
- intrinsic motivation to perform well (mental factors)

When studying **Preparation of the Body** in basketball, your Analysis and Development of Performance will cover all of the *Key Concepts* in this area. As an example of integration, the two Key Concepts of 'physical, skill-related and mental aspects of fitness' and 'principles and methods of training' could link to basketball by including:

- specific physical fitness demands of different roles in basketball (physical fitness)
- reacting quickly to the movements of the opposing team when defending (skill-related fitness)
- applying principles of specificity and progressive overload (principles/methods)
- combining methods of physical and skill-related fitness (principles/methods)

(Other Key Concepts in *Preparation of the Body* would be covered in a similar way.)

Introductory considerations in Analysis and Development of Performance

Your Analysis and Development of Performance work should relate to your Performance improvement work. As you work practically, you will also be learning about relevant Key Concepts in Analysis and Development of Performance.

To help you do this:

- start by identifying your current level of ability (skills/fitness) and your experience of the activity
- keep your practical work closely related to the demands of 'whole' performance
- set the purpose for your practice/game/performance work
- allow time for meaningful performance improvement and understanding of relevant Key Concepts to occur
- build some progression into your practice/game/performance work
- realise that more and more of the same practice is usually not as beneficial as a set of better organised, carefully constructed progressive practices
- have an ongoing review of the practical set-up or 'environment' you are working in – is it useful for what you are intending?

2 BEGINNING YOUR ANALYSIS AND DEVELOPMENT OF PERFORMANCE

The example below shows the link between Performance in volleyball and Analysis of Performance in *Skills and Techniques*: it shows how performing in volleyball links with studying the different Key Concepts in *Skills and Techniques*.

Aims

- **to improve my volleyball performance**
- **to improve my understanding of Skills and Techniques**

Process

Performance (in action)	Analysis of Performance (understanding)
Using skills at the right time. Showing control/fluency in different skills.	Concept of Skill and Skilled Performance
Movement Analysis of my performance	Movement Analysis
	The development of skill and the refinement of technique:
'Parts of skills became automatic as I got better.'	· stages of learning
'Gradual build-up was a useful practice for improving my volley.'	· methods of practice
'I used progression in the different practices in order to keep getting better.'	· principles of effective practice
'My teacher let me know how well I was doing at different practices.'	· the importance of feedback, concentration and motivation

Outcome

- **improved volleyball performance**
- **improved understanding of Skills and Techniques**

The Cycle of Analysis

The Cycle of Analysis is one popular approach that is useful for analysing and developing your performance as part of your performance improvement programme. Using the Cycle of Analysis, you collect information about your performance in an organised way. In this way you identify and assess specific aspects of your performance.

Study the four stages of the Cycle of Analysis in diagram 1. These four stages can be applied effectively to your own activities. Diagram 2 shows the complete cycle of analysis.

By using the Cycle of Analysis, you can continue to improve your performance and so avoid reaching a **learning plateau** – a stage of no apparent progress.

You should design training programmes that allow your performance to show consistent progress. This is better than inconsistent improvement caused by learning plateaux. Diagram 3 outlines how applying the Cycle of Analysis can lead to ongoing improvement in performance.

The diagram below shows the four stages of the Cycle of Analysis.

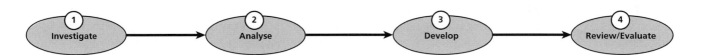

The diagram below outlines how the Cycle of Analysis is formed.

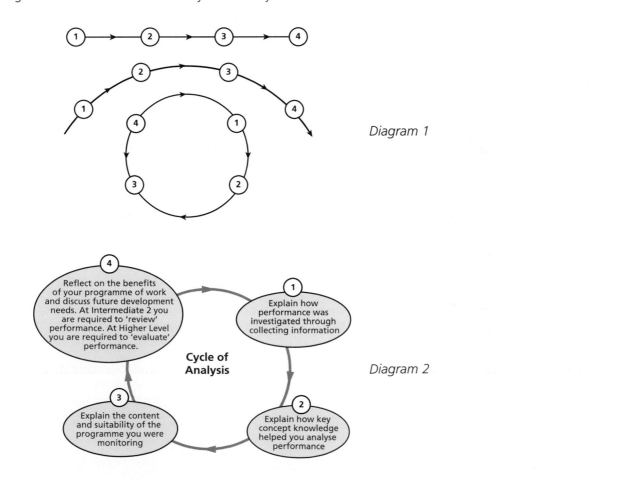

Diagram 1

Diagram 2

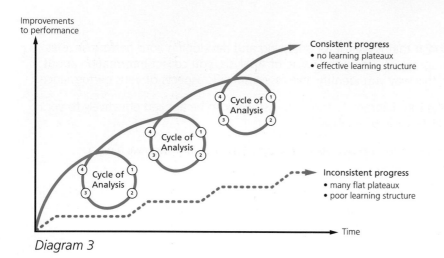

Diagram 3

The intention is to link the **process** of analysing your performance to the **content knowledge** within the Key Concepts. It is useful to consider how you might develop **depth** in your Analysis of Performance answers. Diagram 4 below shows how this can be achieved.

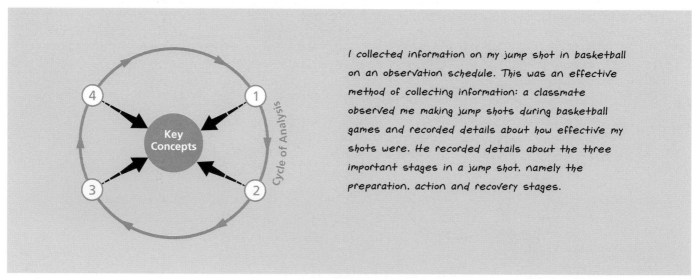

I collected information on my jump shot in basketball on an observation schedule. This was an effective method of collecting information: a classmate observed me making jump shots during basketball games and recorded details about how effective my shots were. He recorded details about the three important stages in a jump shot, namely the preparation, action and recovery stages.

Diagram 4

Diagram 4 represents a student who has a clear grasp of Analysis of Performance processes (the wheel's rim) and who has successfully linked his or her answer to some relevant details within the Key Concepts (the wheel's hub).

In addition, depth in your answers can be added by ensuring that you are familiar with content detail. Diagram 5 on the opposite page represents how this can be achieved.

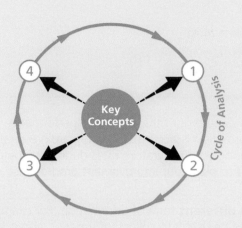

It is important that any information I collected on my performance was specific to me. This was achieved through considering my level of ability, my level of fitness and, because I am in a team, my specific role. As a point guard in basketball, I often take jump shots. This is because I play around the outside of the key, quite far away from the basket. However, if a good shooting opportunity occurs, I will often take it on if this is a good option for my team.

Diagram 5

Diagram 5 represents a student who has detailed knowledge of the Key Concepts (wheel hub) as well as some relevant understanding of the relevant Analysis of Performance processes involved (wheel rim).

Diagram 6 represents the ideal – a student who understands the importance of the relevant Analysis of Performance process and the importance of relevant content knowledge equally. Aim for success by combining the two in your answers and link your practical experience and content knowledge together through the spokes in a wheel. As you move round the Cycle of Analysis (the wheel's rim) you make links with the Key Concepts (the wheel's hub) that are important in the development of your Performance, as shown by the double-headed arrows.

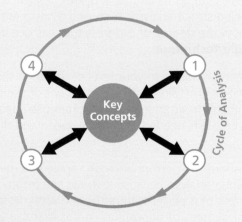

I collected information on my jump shot in basketball on an observation schedule. This was an effective method of collecting information: a classmate observed me making jump shots during basketball games and recorded details about how effective my shots were. He recorded details about the three important stages in a jump shot, namely the preparation, action and recovery stages.

It is important that any information I collected on my performance was specific to me. This was achieved through considering my level of ability, my level of fitness and, because I am in a team, my specific role. As a point guard in basketball, I often take jump shots. This is because I play around the outside of the key, quite far away from the basket. However, if a good shooting opportunity occurs, I will often take it on if this is a good option for my team.

Diagram 6

BEGINNING YOUR ANALYSIS AND DEVELOPMENT OF PERFORMANCE

Methods of collecting information

Collecting valid information is essential. The information you collect must:

- be **specific** to your performance and to your performance level
- **relate** to your Analysis and Development of Performance areas

For example, if you are a very competent footballer, information about your fitness for your performance will come from a competitive situation. This will ensure that the information is **accurate**. If your cardiorespiratory fitness is being measured, the information is collected by measuring your respiratory rates during competitive play. This information about your performance can then be used to plan your improvement programme.

To design a skills-based training programme you would collect a **different** form of information. For example, if you were looking at your effectiveness in passing then it would be useful to collect information about the timing, accuracy, disguise and weight of your different passes. If you were evaluating your team's performance from a strategy perspective, you would collect another different form of information.

You can collect information by using: observation schedules, videos of performances, reflections on your performance, knowledge of results, using a dictaphone, error detection/correction and game analysis.

Observation Schedules

Observation schedules record information about your performance. You are observed performing and a record of your performance is made. Developing the criteria against which your performance is going to be judged is the most important initial consideration. The evidence that you gain from performance has to be **valid**, **reliable** and **straightforward to interpret**.

Study the two examples of observation schedules on pages 15 and 16. The first example on page 15 looks at the effectiveness of someone playing an overhead clear shot in badminton. Repeated observation of the performer allows the observer to make a record of the performer's strengths and weaknesses, relative to the criteria. The criteria are quite specific and this allows for a detailed stroke analysis. A second assessment at a later date against the same criteria can then be recorded to show the degree of progress that has occurred. This format is particularly useful for measuring and analysing a **single technique**.

With this format, you need to ensure that the performance setting is suited to your level of ability. In this example, this would usually mean that you were playing against or practising with an opponent of similar ability. This helps add to the accuracy of the results. If this is difficult to arrange, you can often use a teacher or classmate. She could then feed the shuttlecock to exactly where it is needed and at the speed and direction required for you to collect valid information.

The second example on page 16 shows information collected about the performance of a spike in a game of volleyball. This format for collecting information is useful for game analysis because it shows the results of each spike played. Information from this schedule enables analysis of a player's strengths and weaknesses from different sets, for different angles of spike and against different degrees of opposition. In this example you start from the top of the schedule and record relevant details. First you enter whether or not the point was won from the spike (i.e. was it effective or ineffective?). Then further definition is added: you record information about the angle of the spike, the degree of opposition and the type of set provided. As a result of this observation, you can gain an accurate portrayal of a player's effectiveness in spiking.

Scotstown Academy
Intermediate 2 and Higher Level Physical Education – Observation Schedule
Technique Analysis to identify Strengths/Weaknesses

Date: 25/11/05 Venue: Sports hall Assessor: Steven Turnbull S6 Role: Classmate, Badminton doubles partner
Performance Context: This checklist was completed during competitive practice with a classmate of
similar ability called Zanab Patel. During specified drills my overhead clear was assessed in a 1 hour session.

SKILL: _____Defensive Shot_____ TECHNIQUE: _____Overhead Clear_____

Essential Features	Model Performer	Self Date 1	Self Date 2	Additional comments
PREPARATION				
1. Move to get sideways on	✓	?	✓	
2. Complete backswing of racket	✓	✓	✓	
3. Non-hitting hand points at shuttle	✓	?	✓	
4. Weight over back foot	✓	✗	?	
5. Watch shuttle closely	✓	✓	✓	
ACTION				
1. Wide range of shoulder movement	✓	✓	✓	
2. Speed of racket head – power in shot	✓	✓	✓	
3. Transfer of weight onto front foot	✓	✗	?	
4. Arm straightened to hit shuttle	✓	?	?	
5. Elbow leading hitting action	✓	?	?	
RECOVERY				
1. Follow through in the direction of shuttle	✓	✓	✓	
2. Move forward to mid-court	✓	✗	?	
3. Weight evenly balanced on balls of feet	✓	?	✓	
4. Racket in central ready position	✓	?	✓	
5. Anticipating next shot	✓	✗	?	

Criteria to Be used for assessing performance
✓ = highly bffective – fluent, controlled, etc.
? = limited effectiveness – needs improvement
✗ = ineffective – needs considerable improvement

Scotstown Academy
Intermediate 2 and Higher Level Physical Education – Observation Schedule Technique Analysis to identify Strengths/Weaknesses

Date: 25/11/05 Venue: <u>School sports hall</u> Assessor: <u>Ms M McDonald</u> Role: <u>Teacher</u>
Performance Context: This checklist was completed during an inter-school tournament. The games were 4 v 4 games which allowed many spikes to be attempted.

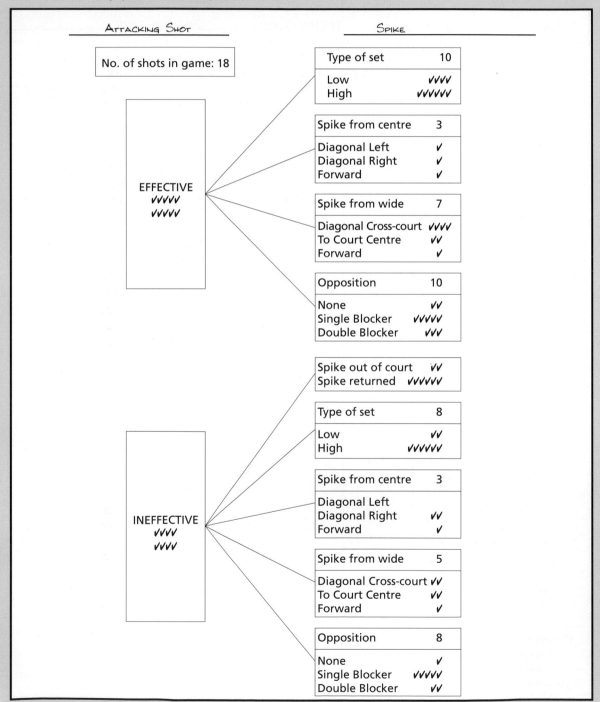

ATTACKING SHOT   SPIKE

No. of shots in game: 18

EFFECTIVE
✓✓✓✓✓
✓✓✓✓✓

Type of set	10
Low	✓✓✓✓
High	✓✓✓✓✓✓

Spike from centre	3
Diagonal Left	✓
Diagonal Right	✓
Forward	✓

Spike from wide	7
Diagonal Cross-court	✓✓✓✓
To Court Centre	✓✓
Forward	✓

Opposition	10
None	✓✓
Single Blocker	✓✓✓✓✓
Double Blocker	✓✓✓

Spike out of court	✓✓
Spike returned	✓✓✓✓✓✓

INEFFECTIVE
✓✓✓✓
✓✓✓✓

Type of set	8
Low	✓✓
High	✓✓✓✓✓✓

Spike from centre	3
Diagonal Left	
Diagonal Right	✓✓
Forward	✓

Spike from wide	5
Diagonal Cross-court	✓✓
To Court Centre	✓✓
Forward	✓

Opposition	8
None	✓
Single Blocker	✓✓✓✓✓
Double Blocker	✓✓

Give three reasons why an observation schedule can be a useful method for collecting information.

Video of Performances

A video recording of a performance is very useful for compiling evidence because it allows you to view a performance repeatedly, and often in slow motion. Slow motion replay is a considerable advantage when the speed of a performance makes recording observations at normal speeds difficult: slowing down the fast and complex action of the tennis serve, for example, allows you to make a detailed technique analysis.

You could use a video recording of your performance to help you complete an observation schedule. For example, your performance as a centre in rugby when kicking from defence could be video recorded and then analysed using an observation schedule.

A video recording of your own or another's performance enables you to observe movements more accurately. Remember to consider the position and angle from which you are collecting video information to ensure that it is useful. This allows you to identify clearly the strengths and weaknesses of the performance.

Reflections on Your Performance

Subjective feelings about performance are also very important. Reflecting on your own performance can often support evidence collected from other sources. You could do this if you felt that your level of fitness was restricting your improvement in performance or if you felt that your ability to apply certain strategies in a game contributed to your success.

Your subjective thoughts and feelings can also be used as information collected about your performance. There are many occasions when strictly objective-based information is not required. For example, in the development of a modern dance motif or a gymnastic sequence, your subjective feelings about the qualities of your performance could best be described by personal reflection. This is because the design of your improvement programme is likely to be open-ended (i.e. you are not following a set formula). Instead, you are using your **imagination** and **critical reflection** to work out ways to enhance your performance. You should keep a record of your thoughts and reflections, e.g. in a performance diary, in order to be able to refer to them.

 Explain the difference between objective and subjective information.

Knowledge of Results

Knowledge of results is also very useful as a measurement of performance. You can use information about results in all four areas of Analysis and Development of Performance.

For example, knowledge of results about success rates in short corners in hockey is useful when discussing both *Skills and Techniques*, and *Structures, Strategies and Composition*. The information collected could relate to success rates at completing the different passing and hitting techniques. It could also relate to information about the strengths and weaknesses of using different players in different positions at short corners. In these examples, using **knowledge of previous performances** is an important part of collecting knowledge of results information.

Knowledge of results can also be useful for collecting information about *Preparation of the Body* (e.g. your level of cardiorespiratory endurance). In most games a high level of cardiorespiratory endurance is required to cope with the high work rate of the body over long periods of time. Monitoring your heart rate provides information about your level of cardiorespiratory fitness.

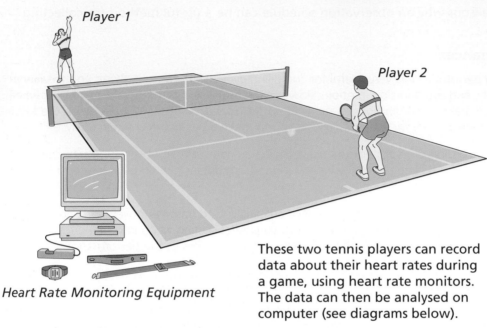

Heart Rate Monitoring Equipment

These two tennis players can record data about their heart rates during a game, using heart rate monitors. The data can then be analysed on computer (see diagrams below).

Data from player 1's Heart Rate Monitor showing effective training

Data from player 2's Heart Rate Monitor showing poor training

If your work rate drops during the later stages of a game, your heart rate also drops. Knowing these figures can help you plan a training programme related to the specific cardiorespiratory demands of the performance. Collected evidence could then be matched to your training zone as shown in the diagram opposite. Improvements in your level of cardiorespiratory fitness could be measured against previous performances in games.

Using a Dictaphone

Using a dictaphone is another effective method of collecting information about your performance. This method is useful as it allows you to immediately record your thoughts with minimal interruption. It can sometimes interrupt the flow of your performance if you pause for too long a time. Hence, a dictaphone is helpful as it allows you to capture some significant specific comments about your performance in a short unfussy way. It is also useful as it allows you to listen to the replays of the tape when it suits you.

Error Detection/Correction

After an initial observation of your performance it is useful for you (on your own or with your teacher) to analyse your performance over a period of time. This will help you evaluate your performance and establish whether your performance is becoming more accurate and consistent. Analysing performance over a period of time helps identify whether there are **specific errors** within your performance which require to be corrected.

Name: Denise Scott   **Date:** 25/11/05

Qualities needed	Court movement criteria	Teacher comment 1st assessment	Teacher comment 2nd assessment
Posture and balance	Body is well centred in preparation for moving	Sometimes your movements begin when you have not established a clear base position	Getting better – still some need to get a little lower and flexed
	Moves early to play shuttle in all directions	Taking smaller initial steps would help balance when moving	Beginning to move away from base in a better posture, especially backwards
	Neat tidy footwork	Footwork is better when a few steps are linked together	Again better when steps are linked
	Body is relaxed, flexed and ready to move	Slightly tense look at times	Looking more relaxed when you have time
Starting and stopping	Can accelerate quickly from a standing start going forwards	Movement is quite fast – greater control is needed	Good, fast – getting more control
	Can accelerate quickly from a standing start going backwards	Slightly arched back leading to poor starting position	Much better. You're starting to move more effectively through better posture and balance
	Can accelerate quickly from a standing start going sideways	Slightly better moving sideways	Again good moving in this direction
	Can remain stable when preparing to play shots	Slightly more open flexed base of support required	Slightly more stable when getting 'set up'
Travelling	Movement in all directions is fluent	Once movement has begun some fluency is evident	Movement again is good when travelling
	Has 'soft feet' when moving	Large steps sometimes lead to 'loud' long steps	Better balance when travelling – good
Lunge and recovery	Can reach and stretch in balance to play shots	Long reach is helping you to recover shots	Reach as ever is good
	Can transfer weight backwards to recover	Slightly slow at beginning your transfer of weight to get back to centre of court	Recovery time is getting better especially when returning from he back of the court
	Teacher comment		

BEGINNING YOUR ANALYSIS AND DEVELOPMENT OF PERFORMANCE

Diagram 7

Details of the agility runs and times completed on court

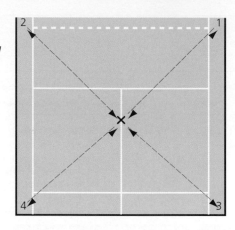

Diagram 8

	1st attempt	2nd attempt	3rd attempt	1st attempt average	2nd attempt average
1. Base (x) to front forehand corner at start of training	3.7 s	3.8 s	3.9 s	3.8 s	
1. Base to front forehand corner at end of training	3.5 s	3.5 s	3.8 s		3.6 s
2. Base to front backhand corner at start of training	3.8 s	3.6 s	4.1 s	3.9 s	
2. Base to front backhand corner at end of training	3.6 s	3.6 s	3.9 s		3.7 s
3. Base to back forehand corner at start of training	4.0 s	3.9 s	4.3 s	4.1 s	
3. Base to back forehand corner at end of training	3.8 s	3.7 s	3.9 s		3.8 s
4. Base to back backhand corner at start of training	4.2 s	4.3 s	4.1 s	4.2 s	
4. Base to back backhand corner at end of training	3.8 s	3.8 s	3.8 s		3.8 s

Diagram 7 highlights the performance qualities and criteria required for effective court movement in badminton. The teacher comments compiled for the second assessment have detected that the overall performance weakness (error) is the student's difficulty with their posture and balance. The student still needs to get a little lower and flexed. From this error detection analysis a number of correction remedies are possible. This could involve: repeating again the same analysis with further teacher commentary at a later date; defining further qualitative performance criteria for more detailed error detection analysis of posture and balance or alternatively completing a quantitative measurement of performance. This might be useful, as it would enable a combination of qualitative and quantitative data to be collected.

Diagram 8 is an example of how this could be completed for effective court movement in badminton. Completing these agility-based movement practices would indicate whether the effect that posture and balance (along with other performance qualities) was having on your court speed was improving or not.

 Explain why collecting initial and then focused data about your performance can be effective in the analysis and development of performance.

Game Analysis

Game analysis is a useful way of using statistical information to analyse performance. In the example below a range of general and specific information is available which can 'paint a picture' of how previous tennis matches between two players have been decided.

With this type of information you should be able to analyse your own performance in ways which relate to all the different areas of Analysis and Development of Performance.

- Within *Performance Appreciation*, information about your second serve effectiveness and number of double faults might highlight whether any particular mental factors were influencing your performance. A high return rate would indicate that you are able to manage your emotions well and a low return rate might indicate some anxiety in your performance.

- Within *Preparation of the Body*, first services 'in' and first service points won is an indicator of different aspects of fitness: physical fitness (power); skill-related fitness (timing) and mental aspects of fitness (rehearsal). Sustained first service effectiveness indicates that your overall fitness is high and low service speeds indicate otherwise.

- Within *Skills and Techniques*, analysis of the different stroke techniques (volleys, drives, smash) indicates the relative strengths and weaknesses of your overall tennis performance.

- Within S*tructures, Strategies and Composition*, an analysis of your tactics through considering the percentage of shots which were won at the net or from the baseline are useful in highlighting whether you were playing the type of game you considered when preparing for the game.

Tennis: Game analysis

Player A		Performance Criterion		Player B	
1.75m		Height		1.83m	
		Weight			
Right-handed		Plays		Left-handed	
		Previous Matches			
Year	**Tournament**	**Surface**	**Stage**	**Winner**	**Score**
2003	Local League	Hard	QF	Player A	4-6, 6-3, 6-3
2004	Club Championship	Grass	SF	Player B	6-2, 6-4
2004	Regional League	Carpet	Final	Player A	6-3, 4-6, 6-2
		Detailed analysis of last game			
		Service			
58%		1st serves in		64%	
86%		2nd serves in		84%	
12		Aces		17	
5		Double faults		6	
75%		1st serve points won		78%	
55%		2nd serve points won		48%	
		Returns			
64%		All returns in		58%	
66%		Forehand returns in		62%	
62%		Backhand returns in		54%	
		Tactics			
52%		Points won at net		58%	
55%		Points won from baseline		48%	
		Strokes			
4		Volley winners		7	
2		Smash winners		4	
8		Passing winners		2	
4		Lob winners		1	

3 AREA 1 PERFORMANCE APPRECIATION

Key concepts in Performance Appreciation

• **Overall nature and demands of quality performance**

• **Technical, physical, personal and special qualities of performance**

• **Mental factors influencing performance**

• **Use of appropriate models of performance**

• **Planning and managing personal performance improvement**

Area	Performance Appreciation
Key Concept 1	Overall nature and demands of quality performance

In this Key Concept you **examine in detail** the nature of quality performance and the different demands of performance.

People participate in different sporting activities for many varied reasons. The nature and demands of each sporting activity interest people in different ways. Your own favourite sporting activities may appeal to you in some of the ways outlined in the diagram below. This diagram shows some **general** performance considerations.

 Can you think of other activities that have for you a special nature, special challenges, a quality focus or experiential nature?

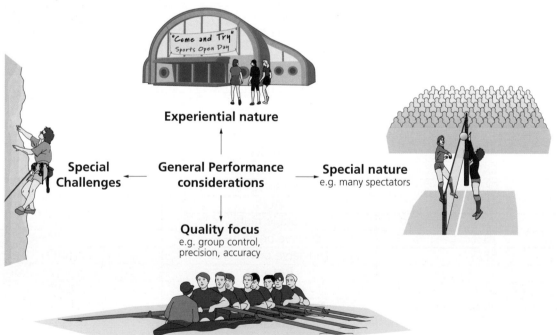

Experiential nature

Special Challenges ← General Performance considerations → Special nature
e.g. many spectators

Quality focus
e.g. group control, precision, accuracy

The demands of Performance involves recognising that quality performance depends on considering other factors, which characterise activities. This includes whether activities are: individual, team or group activities, competitive or non competitive and the rules, codes, conduct and scoring systems which define activities.

 Explain the overall nature and demands of the activities in your course.

Area	Performance Appreciation
Key Concept 2	Technical, physical, personal and special qualities of performance

In this Key Concept you **examine in detail** the qualities required in evaluating the strengths and weaknesses of individual, team or group performance.

Once you have reviewed the general nature and demands of performance it is useful to analyse **specific** performance qualities. The diagram below gives examples of different **special, personal, technical** and **physical** qualities.

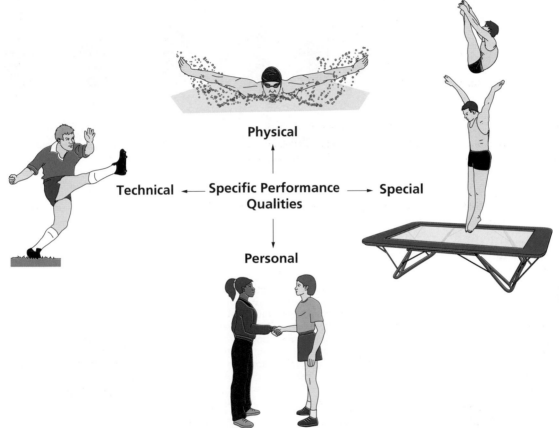

As your appreciation of performance develops, you can analyse the role of different qualities involved in your performance. Any **'whole' performance** is likely to involve many different qualities with some more important than others.

For example, a trampolinist may display **special qualities** of invention in the ways in which different parts of the sequence have been composed. These may be based on a change in body alignment, axis of rotation and speed of different movements, all of which make the routine creative and expressive. However, it is likely that a trampolinist also shows **technical quality** by being able to carry out some bounce control and different turns and twists in the air, which shows refinement, timing and an ability to complete challenging moves in a consistent and effective way. In addition, it is likely that a trampolinist shows **personal qualities**, for example, determination and courage in taking on new challenging moves. It is likely, as well, that they are highly motivated to succeed. **Physical qualities** of both power and lightness of touch (in being able to relax then drive upwards and forcefully from the trampoline) are also likely to be evident.

 Explain the technical, physical, personal and special qualities of performance qualities you used in different activities in your course.

The article below outlines how different qualities are required in most activities. The article is about a triathlete competing in the Sydney Olympics in 2000 and it highlights that much more than physical fitness is required in this demanding event. Study the article below and try to recognise the different qualities required in a triathlete.

'THE LEGS LET DOWN THE INTELLECT'
by Richard Williams,
The Guardian, 18/9/2000

When Simon Lessing crossed the finish line hardly anyone was watching him. The red-hot favourite for the first triathlon gold medal ever awarded at the Olympic Games had finished 60sec behind the winner. After 11 years as a triathlete and with four world championships behind him, Lessing was not about to show whatever disappointment he may have been feeling at finishing a mere ninth. And within a few minutes of tasting defeat Lessing had recovered his composure and was analyzing the experience with cool clarity. 'I'm a marked man out there' he said, 'which means that people are always focusing their race around what I'm doing'.

Lessing is a mature and sophisticated 29 year old who has accumulated the strength, both physical and mental, to cope with the challenge of a contest which features a 1.5km swim in open water, a 40km bicycle ride and a 10km foot race, altogether lasting a shade over an hour and three-quarters. But there was a shade of resentment, perhaps unavoidable, in his voice as he spoke of the tactics employed by the medal winners. 'Of course it's very easy just to sit at the back of the pack' he said. 'The guys who did well we never saw in front. When you do that the choice is to let the race happen in front of you and hope to be lucky'.

Where the triathlon really differs from other multi-disciplinary sports, is not, as one might expect, in the need for sheer strength and endurance but in the depth of its tactical demands. At this level the real battle in the triathlon is between the athletes' intellects.

No one is equally strong in the water, on the bike and on foot. Each competitor must plot his own performance curve, building in a measure of compensation for his weaknesses while bearing in mind a need to shadow his rivals or to lure them into overreaching themselves. Someone who finishes the swim with a lead of half a minute may already have a shrewd idea that they will not be finishing the race in the top five.

Lessing had begun the race exactly as he intended, taking a good early position as the 52 competitors began the swim. He finished the swim in second place. In the cycle race, Lessing held a place inside the top 10, doing his share of the work to maintain the pace and neutralize a succession of breaks, but on the penultimate lap Olivier Marceau, the reigning World Champion, showed his French pedigree by jumping into a lead, tracked only by Conrad Stoltz of South Africa. As they leapt off their bikes and into their running shoes they had a minute's lead over the pursuing pack, with Lessing inside the top 10.

But the third and final leg is the triathlon's moment of truth. Of Lessing, known for husbanding his resources for the final push, there was no sign. As soon as he had dismounted from the bike his first few steps told him that the strength had gone from his legs.

But had the pressure, on this day of all days finally got to the apparently unflappable Lessing? 'If you're competing at this level, the pressure is part of the sport' he said. 'Maybe in 2004 the pressure will be off and I can be one of the guys who can take a risk.'

Comparing yourself with top performers is also useful in developing an appreciation of quality performance. Consider these two examples: one from a footballer and one from an athlete.

Some examples of performance qualities have been highlighted. You may be able to identify others.

'SALUTE THE REIGN OF KING HENRY'

by Hugh McIlvanney,
The Sunday Times,
30/11/2003

Of course Thierry Henry should be named World Player of the Year. It seems to me impossible to argue that any footballer is currently bringing more talent, excitement and effectiveness to his performances. For several seasons now, his standards have been undeniably phenomenal.

That is why the really interesting debate goes beyond the issue of where the Arsenal man stands in the game today and into the tricky but intriguing assessments of how he compares with the greatest goal-scoring front players in living memory.

I am bound to suggest that Henry's ranking must be high, since I think he is one of the best-equipped attackers I have ever seen. Naturally it helps to clarify the case for him if we accept the need to narrow the terms of the comparison. Among the ultimate greats of offensive play, Pele, Diego Maradona and Johan Cruyff had a much wider range of responsibilities in their teams than Henry, who – for all the impressive variety of his penetrative manoeuvres, and his habit of making goals for teammates – is always unmistakably a striker.

When anybody waxes lyrical about Henry's combination of divine grace and deadliness,

George Best is deservedly mentioned as the very incarnation of those qualities. However, though Best hit the net with outrageous frequency he perhaps should be left out of our immediate considerations because he was a winger. In fact,

there was scarcely any limit to his magical capacities, but if we are to keep the comparative process manageable, the figures we evoke to set aside Henry must be strikers.

That criterion would put Denis Law in the frame. Technically, he was inferior to the Frenchman, whose striking of the ball is infinitely purer than Law's ever was. However, Law possessed bottomless courage, supernatural sharpness of reaction, positional cunning and wonderful timing. Law was a miracle of suddenness when it counted.

The predatory tradition at Manchester United is being

splendidly maintained by Ruud Van Nistelrooy and there are many around Old Trafford and elsewhere who rate the Dutch goal-machine as more valuable than Henry. I believe the extra fluency, expansiveness and adaptability of Henry gives him the edge. One son of Holland who could rival Henry in those areas of ability was Marco Van Basten whose feats for Ajax, AC Milan and the national team in the 1980's and 1990's have presented persuasive evidence that he was the greatest of all strikers.

For sheer ruthless finishing, surely nobody could match the German Gerd Muller, who, in a career spanning the 1960's and 1970's, was almost irresistible for Bayern Munich and his country. His 62 caps yielded 68 goals, a strike-rate that makes the mind reel. But, while I thrilled to Muller's skills in the box, it was Van Basten who imprinted the more glittering images on my memory. Van Basten could both flow and explode, exploiting exceptional close control, two-footed shooting and excellence in the air with athletic authority, keen intelligence and remarkable composure under pressure. I did not expect to see an equal. Now Henry threatens that assumption. His effortlessly delicate touch in receiving and running with the ball, his sublime balance and the booster-rocket acceleration with which he leaves defenders adrift are all applied with relaxed confidence.

Comparisons are entertaining but the best way to react to Thierry Henry is to celebrate him as a glorious original. For me, he is as

- An example of **technical** quality is 'his effortlessly delicate touch in receiving and running with the ball, his sublime balance'.

- An example of **physical** quality is 'the booster-rocket acceleration with which he leaves defenders adrift'.

- An example of **personal** quality is 'it seems to me impossible to argue that any footballer is currently bringing more talent, excitement and effectiveness to his performances'.

- An example of **special** quality is 'the extra fluency, expansiveness and adaptability of Henry gives him the edge'.

'BRAVE RADCLIFFE RULES THE WORLD WITHOUT DOUBT'

by Simon Barnes,
The Times, 14/4/2003

Radcliffe's time of 2hr 15mins 25secs beat her own world record, set last Autumn in Chicago, by nearly two minutes. She beat her nearest rival yesterday by 4¼ minutes. She led from start to finish and no woman got even close to her.

When you say she won by miles, it is almost the literal truth – that four minute plus margin represents a distance not much short of a full mile. And this was the woman who once seemed doomed to be the world's pluckiest loser, the one who did all the hard work in the Olympic 10,000 metres in Sydney and then got out-sprinted to finish in fourth place. She lacked the pace you see. Lacked the judgement. Lacked the heart. Less than two years ago, she ran the 10,000 metres at the World Championships and guess where she finished? Fourth again.

Poor Paula! We all felt sorry for her and wondered when we would get the next session of Paula and her doomed heroics. Where did it come from, this self-belief, this lust for conquest? It all began at the London Marathon last year, when she ran away from the field, leaving television commentators quacking their dismay, saying it was impossible to maintain such a pace. It was, too – so Paula went faster. And faster. She went on to set her marathon world record later the same year.

The all-too-vulnerable Paula is now invincible. She was expected to win yesterday, she was expected to set a world record and she confounded expectation only by doing so by such extreme margins. It was above all, a run of blazing confidence, of blinding self-belief. It was the self-certainty of a woman whose time – whose distance – had come. The run was 'a good reflection of the training I put in' she said, meaning that the confidence and belief is grounded in the knowledge of a perfect preparation. This knowledge destroys the self-doubt of the bad bits, the painful bits and there is no marathon without pain. Her method for coping with this is natural – she counts. Three lots of 100 and another mile has been knocked on the head. 'That way I think only of the minute I am in', she said.

Radcliffe's great skill is her ability to 'run as I feel'. That is to say, she has a profound knowledge of her own capabilities, an ability to read how she is feeling at any one moment with objective accuracy and to correlate this with her potential. To complete this journey at all is a spectacular achievement, but Radcliffe has done it in record time.

- An example of **technical** quality is 'Radcliffe's great skill is her ability to "run as I feel".

- An example of **physical** quality is 'the run was "a good reflection of the training I put in".

- An example of **personal** quality is 'it was above all, a run of blazing confidence'.

- An example of **special** quality is 'she has a profound knowledge of her own capabilities, an ability to read how she is feeling at any one moment with objective accuracy and to correlate this with her potential'.

Area	Performance Appreciation
Key Concept 3	Mental factors influencing performance

In this **Key Concept** you **examine in detail** the importance of managing your emotions before/during/after performance and studying different methods for improving the management of your emotions.

In addition to general performance considerations and specific performance qualities, it is useful to study some of the **mental** factors that influence your performance, especially during 'whole' performance.

These include **motivation, confidence and concentration** and the fine detail of **body preparation**. Motivation, confidence and concentration are covered in detail on pages 75 to 78. The *Preparation of the Body* section on pages 34 to 56 includes some further consideration of mental aspects of fitness as well as practice considerations for mental training.

From the two articles referred to on pages 25 and 26, it is apparent that these top performers are able to control their stress levels and manage their emotions in very demanding performances. This allows them to work '**at the limit**' of their potential. It also allows them to be comfortable when performing. Top performers often appear to have more time than other performers and can work within their '**comfort zone**'.

To bring about improvements to your self-management you have to want it to happen. Change can often be difficult. Factors such as how you use your time, degree of effort, having a positive attitude and taking personal responsibility are all likely to be important.

You may have experienced performances in which your mental state **helped** your performance. You may also have experienced performances in which your mental state **hindered** your performance. Identifying those factors which you can control and attempting to improve them is a useful starting point.

Five factors that influence your mental state during your performance are **anxiety**, **self-confidence**, **level of arousal**, **codes of conduct** and **the importance of the particular event/competition**.

 Write down examples from your own performances in different activities of times that you feel you have performed 'within your comfort zone' and/or 'at the limit' of your potential. Check your answer with classmates and your teacher.

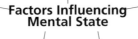

Self-confidence

Usually a self-confident performer will take on options that may present themselves. (e.g. taking a sudden shot in football rather than passing and avoiding the responsibility of shooting).

Importance of event/competition

You may perform well on big occasions; others may find that it adds to their stress levels.

Factors Influencing Mental State

Level of arousal

Positive levels of arousal (a feeling of excitement) can help performance. Negative arousal (a feeling of apprehension) can hinder your performance. Likewise, having control over your level of aggression as necessary will be a performance advantage and not controlling your level of aggression will be a disadvantage.

Anxiety

Occasionally you can 'feel' threatened when performing (e.g. a golf drive with 'out of bounds' to one side).

Codes of conduct

In football it is important that you play according to the formal rules and expectations of fair football. This involves using force when tackling for the ball but avoids using excessive unnecessary force.

3 AREA 1 PERFORMANCE APPRECIATION

Developing positive feelings about your performance and overcoming negative thoughts about your performance are important in managing your emotions and reducing any unnecessary performance anxiety.

Imagery (including visualisation) is a useful technique for considering in detail your performance goals and relaxation techniques (including deep breathing exercises) are useful for helping you achieve your performance goals.

Imagery

As with other aspects of performance, imagery requires practice if it is to benefit the development of your performance. For most effective results you require to have a positive self image of what effective performance would look and feel like. To help you, try to picture (**visualise**) images of your performance in fine detail. Imagery also includes other details of performance. As well as visual imagery you should try to make use of other senses (touching, hearing) to enhance performance. Practise for a short amount of time (a few minutes) in a quiet area.

To reinforce your image of performance you can write out 'your picture' of performance. This can be refined as your performance develops.

Example – Volleyball set

Components: Movement anticipation, footwork, control, recovery

Image description: Watch the player who is passing to you closely. Move quickly with light agile footwork. Lower your centre of gravity by dropping your upper body. As you get to where the ball is anticipated to land, you should move your arms up ready to intercept the ball. Take small steps on final approach. Relax your shoulders. Absorb the ball with your hands and arms and control your action and the ball's reaction through taking a light touch of the ball. Your setting should be quiet and controlled. You should hear little apart from the sound of the ball gently resting in the cup of your hands for a split second. Watch the ball all the way through your movement and get ready to recover your hands for setting again.

Refine: Rewrite the script until you are executing the set as you wish.

Relaxation techniques

Developing the ability to 'relax' can be useful for rest and recovery during competition, for example, between badminton games in a competition. It is also useful for helping you to prepare for activity when you combine relaxation techniques with imagery exercises. Relaxation techniques can release tension in muscles and help you to control breathing.

To purposefully 'relax' lie down quietly in a comfortable position and close your eyes. Breathe in a steady deep rhythm through your nose and become aware of your breathing. Continue for a few minutes. When you finish, lie quietly for a further few minutes, closed eyes at first then with opened eyes. If your mind wanders try to relax again through concentrating on your breathing rhythm.

 Quicksmart: Explain techniques you have used to develop positive feelings about your performance in different activities in your course.

 Quicksmart: Explain different mental factors which have helped and hindered your performance in different activities in your course.

Area	Performance Appreciation
Key Concept 4	Use of appropriate models of performance

In this **Key Concept** you **examine in detail** the relevance of **comparing** and **contrasting** model performers and the importance of **using different methods for collecting feedback** to compare performance with model performance.

Comparing and contrasting your performance with a model performer is a good way to establish your training priorities at the beginning, during and conclusion of your planned improvement programme. The observation checklist on page 15 makes comparisons with a model performer for this reason.

Model performers exist at different levels of ability. Comparing your ability with a classmate, whose abilities are close to the class average, may sometimes be useful for establishing your own relative strengths and weaknesses. At other times, in other activities, it may be useful to compare your performance with a performer of a higher level of ability, for example a student competing at a national level in a sport. At other times an even higher level of performer may be necessary for comparison.

Analysing model performers can be very useful for appreciating in detail all that a performance includes, for example, information about the fitness needs of performance, the exact requirements of different skills and the effectiveness of your decision-making.

An Example from Tennis

Analysing model performers can also show how performance is developing and changing within an activity. For example, a new technique called the power forehand has been developed by top tennis players. The aim is to hit the ball both earlier and harder in order to put your opponent under greater pressure. The diagram on page 30 illustrates the main differences between the conventional and the power forehand.

Analysis of and comparison with model performers can highlight all the performance demands of this new power forehand stroke. For example, this new technique has significant physical fitness demands. Players using this new technique often undertake new forms of physical fitness training such as rebound training (plyometrics) and upper body strength training programmes to ensure that they can perform this new technique safely even when under pressure in a long game.

Conventional Forehand

Grip - Continental grip with hand over top of racquet

Stance - Closed stance with shoulder leading shot

Racquet Swing - Racquet finishes pointing over net

Ball Strike - Hit at or below waist height as ball drops with little spin

Knee Position - Shot hit with knees bent

Feet Position - Ball hit with at least one foot on the ground

Power Forehand

Grip - Grip with hand underneath racquet

Stance - Open stance with 'coiling' of upper body

Racquet Swing - Racquet finishes above opposite shoulder and pointing behind the player

Ball Strike - Hit at shoulder height with lots of topspin while ball still rising

Knee Position - Strong upward knee thrust into shot with legs fully extended

Feet Position - Ball hit with both feet off the ground

Useful methods for collecting feedback to compare performance with model performance include the following:

- knowledge of results
- knowledge of previous performance
- error detection/correction
- personal reflection
- use of video/dictaphone

How you use these different methods for collecting information to provide effective feedback about performance is covered in detail on pages 14 to 20.

 What information have you collected through comparing your performance with a model performer in different activities in your course?

Area	Performance Appreciation
Key Concept 5	Planning and managing personal performance improvement

In this Key Concept you **examine in detail** the importance of using short- and long-term goals to plan for '**whole performance**' improvements. The importance of personal monitoring, review and evaluation of progress to inform managing your development needs is also considered.

- Goal-setting principles are an important part of planning for performance improvement. Earlier on pages 23 and 26 you have studied why different qualities (technical, physical, personal and special) are often used when evaluating the strengths and weaknesses of individual, team or group performance. Remembering these is useful as they help link the general area of *Performance Appreciation* with the other three specific areas of Analysis and Development of Performance. (More information on this link is provided on pages 8 to 10.)

- Goal-setting principles, for example, could link to **physical** and **mental** fitness aspects of performance as part of your *Preparation of the Body* study. For example, imagery and visualisation are important mental aspects of fitness. In addition, some **special** aspects of performance link to a consideration of the benefits of training for peak performance.

- Goal-setting principles, for example, could link to aspects of *Skills and Techniques*. **Technical** aspects of performance link to skills and techniques as do some personal aspects of performance, such as the importance of motivation.

- Goal-setting principles, for example, could link to aspects of *Structures, Strategies and Composition*. In planning your individual, group or team performance you will require to consider the **personal** qualities you possess as well as tactical and design considerations which are specific to your individual, team or group performance.

Managing your Development Needs

When monitoring, reviewing and evaluating your overall performance it is useful to set performance goals which are based on your current level of ability. Goal-setting is an effective way of helping you understand what your performance targets are. Goals can motivate you towards performance improvement and can also help reduce any anxieties you may have about your performance.

When setting goals, it is useful to follow certain principles. The National Coaching Foundation uses the acronym 'SMARTER' as a way of explaining how best to make goal-setting work for you. The 'SMARTER' acronym is explained fully on the next page.

'SMARTER'

Specific • Make your goals specific to you, your ability and your experience within an activity. Focus on exactly what you wish to improve, for example specific skills within a game.

Measurable • Set measurable targets for improvement. (An example is the target of improving your time in a swimming stroke over a specific distance by a set time.)

Agreed • Agree your goals with your teacher. This allows you to work together with clear and agreed training goals set out.

Realistic • Make your training goals attainable. If they are too ambitious, you may become demoralised. If they are realistic and achievable, you will be motivated to try to achieve your goals.

Time-phased • First achieve your short-term goals. This then leads you to achieve your long-term goals.

Exciting • Be interested in achieving your goals! They need to excite you. Practising for long periods on tasks that are of little interest to you will adversely affect your performance. Make your practices short, sharp and meaningful.

Recorded • Make a record of what your training goals are. Note them down in your training diary or record of work. As your short-term goals are achieved, you can note these in your record of progress.

 Explain the short- and long-term goals you have selected for the different activities in your course.

Course assessment: revision questions

These revision questions are designed to help you improve your content knowledge (the wheel's hub – see page 11 to 13) and to help you check how well you are progressing. Model answers are provided at the back of this book. Most questions can be answered within a few lines but some are a little more demanding and require additional reading to inform your answers.

Tip: Ensure your answers are about your performance in an activity from your course.

Performance Appreciation

1. State some of the ways in which the nature and demands of activities might differ.

2. Quality of performance depends upon many factors. State four different factors.

3. For one activity, describe four different qualities that are important within whole performance.

4. State four different ways it could be evident that you were effectively managing your emotions during a team/group performance.

5. State three different senses you can use to help develop imagery.

6. Describe how you would practise through relaxation techniques to release tension in muscles and control breathing.

7. Give three advantages of comparing yourself with a model performer.

8. Why is it useful to set short-term goals as well as long-term goals?

9. Describe four different criteria that you should consider when setting goals.

10. Quality performance is affected by many factors. Choose four different factors and for each of these give two examples of how these four qualities might benefit your performance. Ensure your answer relates to the same activity. You could set out your analysis like this:

Activity

Quality Performance	Reason
	1 2
	1 2
	1 2
	1 2

11. The following table lists some factors and possible objectives for improving your performance within them. Complete the table by supplying methods of achieving these objectives. You may list more than one method of achieving each objective.

Factors	Objectives for improvement	Methods of achieving objectives
Self confidence	Self talk Task goals Structured competition	
Level of anxiety and arousal	Level of readiness for activity	
Concentration	Selective attention Task demands	

Key Concepts in Preparation of the Body

- Fitness assessment in relation to personal performance and the demands of activities

- Application of different types of fitness in the development of activity specific performance

- Physical, skill-related and mental aspects of fitness

- Principles and methods of training

- Planning, implementing and monitoring training

Area	Preparation of the Body
Key Concept 1	Fitness assessment in relation to personal performance and the demands of activities

In this Key Concept you **examine in detail** how fitness assessment and analysis of test results can contribute to performance training.

To plan performance improvements in different activities it is useful to collect **specific** information about your **overall** fitness. This information can tell you about your physical, skill-related and mental fitness.

Information can be collected from specific fitness tests or through performance in the activity. The purpose of fitness testing is to provide relevant and accurate information on your current fitness strengths and weaknesses. Therefore, it is important that any fitness assessment takes into account the **nature of the activity**, and includes **standardised test procedures** and **regular monitoring of performance**.

Fitness Testing

Initial fitness assessments can be used as your starting information for a fitness training programme. Using the same fitness assessments both **during** and **at the end** of your programme will provide relevant information for comparison.

Most fitness tests are straightforward in their design. This helps to ensure that if you follow all their instructions you will be able to gather relevant and accurate fitness information.

Two examples of cardiorespiratory endurance tests are the Harvard Step Test and the 12-minute Cooper Test.

Harvard Step Test

Aim To use your **recovery rate** from exercise to calculate your level of cardiorespiratory endurance

Equipment A bench to step up onto at 45 cm height

Test Procedure 5 minutes at a rate of 30 step-ups onto the bench per minute

Test Calculation Heart rate taken by pulse checks on three occasions

        1. between 1 min and 1 min 30 s
        2. between 2 min and 2 min 30 s
        3. between 3 min and 3 min 30 s.

The totals from these three recordings are then used to calculate your score using the following formula:

$$\text{Score} = \frac{\text{duration of exercise in seconds}}{\text{pulse count}} \times \frac{100}{1}$$

where pulse count = (2 × [heart rate after 1 minute]) + (2 × [heart rate after 2 minutes]) + (2 × [heart rate after 3 minutes])

Use the table below to measure your performance level.

Performer \ Performance level	High	Above average	Average	Below average	Low
Male 15/16 years	above 90	90–80	79–65	64–55	below 55
Female 15/16 years	above 86	86–76	75–61	60–50	below 50

12-minute Cooper Test

Aim To calculate your level of cardiorespiratory endurance by applying a time/distance formula.

Equipment A flat area, e.g. outdoor field or athletics track

Test Procedure 12 minutes to cover the maximum distance possible through running, jogging or walking

Test Calculation Use the table below to measure your own performance

Performer		Performance Level			
Age	Sex	Excellent	Good	Fair	Poor
13–14 years	male	2700	2400	2200	2100
	female	2000	1900	1600	1500
15–16 years	male	2800	2500	2300	2200
	female	2100	1900	1700	1500
17–18 years	male	3000	3000	2500	2300
	female	2300	2300	1800	1500

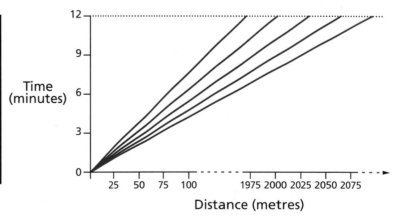

Other types of test

Physical fitness tests exist in all aspects of physical fitness (e.g. sit-and-reach tests for flexibility and vertical jump tests for explosive strength).

Skill-related fitness tests exist as well. For example, the Illinois Agility Run test combines running with many different changes of direction and is a recognised test for agility.

Very often you will use your whole performance for collecting relevant fitness information. This can be a useful method of assessing different types of fitness.

 Why should fitness training information you collect be specific to your performance?

4 AREA 2 PREPARATION OF THE BODY

An example from a football game

This table has been used to collect cardiorespiratory information from a football game.

DATE: 25/11/05				VENUE: School Pitch				OPPOSITION: Scotstown U16							
ROLE IN TEAM: Midfield								LENGTH OF GAME: 90 minutes							
PITCH CONDITIONS: Slightly wet								OVERHEAD CONDITIONS: Dry and Bright							
Walking				Jogging				Mid-pace Running				Sprinting (10 m – 30 m)			
0–22 min	23–45 min	46–68 min	69–90 min	0–22 min	23–45 min	46–68 min	69–90 min	0–22 min	23–45 min	46–68 min	69–90 min	0–22 min	23–45 min	46–68 min	69–90 min
✓✓✓	✓✓✓✓	✓✓✓✓✓	✓✓✓✓✓✓	✓✓✓✓	✓✓	✓✓	✓✓✓✓	✓✓✓✓✓	✓✓✓✓✓✓	✓✓✓✓	✓✓✓	✓✓✓✓✓✓✓✓✓	✓✓✓✓✓✓	✓✓✓✓	✓✓

The table provides valuable information about how well the player was able to walk, jog, mid-pace run and sprint throughout the game. The main evidence from this table is that as the game proceeded the player became slightly more tired. This affected her mid-pace running to a limited extent. However, it affected her ability to sprint to a much greater extent. For example, during the first 22 minutes of the game the player made 9 sprint runs. However, from the 69th to 90th minute of the game, the player only made 2 sprint runs. This physical fitness information has implications for the whole performance. The evidence is that as the player became increasingly tired throughout the game she became less able to sprint. This tiredness affects performance in many ways (for example, in being unable to carry out attacking sprints into open space, and in being less able to cover space when defending).

An example from swimming

It is often useful to use both fitness tests and your whole performance to collect fitness information. In this way the results of your fitness tests can be used to support your whole performance findings.

For example, to measure your degree of dynamic strength improvement in 100 m front crawl, you may want to use the following methods for collecting information:

Whole performance (pool-based) – Swim 100 m front crawl at full speed. Rest for five minutes. Repeat a further three times. Calculate average time.

Fitness tests (land-based) – Sprint for 1 minute (Shuttle runs over 15 m). Rest for five minutes. Repeat a further three times. Calculate average time per shuttle run.

The related fitness tests would provide **objective** information to support any conclusions you may be able to draw from your whole performance results. If your times in both your 100 m front crawl and running times had improved, this would imply that your physical fitness had improved.

 Explain the fitness assessment procedures you have used on your course. Explain how the fitness information you collected was relevant and accurate for the different activities on your course?

It could be that your pool-based times did not improve, but your land-based fitness test results did improve. This would imply that other factors such as your swimming technique had influenced your pool-based times. It would also show that your level of physical fitness had improved.

Another example from swimming

Occasionally you may find it difficult to find exactly enough fitness tests to provide supporting objective information to compare with your whole performance. In this case you would need to measure in detail your physical fitness from your performance in the activity.

The aim of this fitness assessment is to provide information about the **effects of local muscular endurance** on performance in the 400 m front crawl.
Whole performance – Swim 400 m front crawl at 50–60% of maximum speed. (16 × 25 m lengths)

Length numbers	Individual length times (s)	Number of breaths	Number of arm strokes
1/2	24/25	5/6	15/16
3/4	25/26	6/7	16/16
5/6	26/27	7/7	16/17
7/8	28/28	7/8	17/17
9/10	28/28	8/8	17/18
11/12	28/27	8/9	18/19
13/14	29/28	9/9	19/20
5/16	30/29	9/10	20/20

General comment about arm recovery and effectiveness of arm pull in 400 m front crawl: (This information could be gathered after talking with your teacher once she has observed your performance.)

'For the first 10 lengths the arms were pulling effectively and there was a good recovery position achieved. The arms came out of the water and were carried forward, with a high elbow, to an entry point well in front of the swimmer's head. The hand then moved forward underwater before achieving a good strong catch position from an outstretched hand position. Between 11 and 14 lengths it became increasingly difficult to maintain this arm pull and recovery. The arm was coming out from the water at a lower angle and was unable to be carried forward enough for an effective entry position. The position of the elbow was lower. The arm pull was beginning from a bent arm position rather than from an outstretched hand. Lengths 15 to 16 showed increased signs of tiredness with the arm recovery becoming lower and the arm pull less effective.'

Mental Fitness

Most relevant fitness assessments of how mental fitness affects performance would be collected from your whole performance. For example, if you were part of a football team that regularly lost goals very late in a game you might find that this was due to mental fatigue. From this information you could plan effective training to bring about improvements in your team's capacity to focus and concentrate for the entire game.

 For further information about mental factors that influence performance, see page 27 and 28. For further information about mental training principles, see page 52.

4 AREA 2 PREPARATION OF THE BODY

Area	Preparation of the Body
Key Concept 2	Application of different types of fitness in the development of activity specific performance

In this **Key Concept** you **examine in detail** how performance requirements and related fitness needs for selected activities link to specific training.

In attempting to improve your body preparation for performance improvement, different performance-related fitness requirements need to be considered. Many of these are related to following a planned improvement programme. The **Cycle of Analysis** outlined on page 11 is one planned approach you may use.

Performance-related fitness includes setting **specific performance objectives** for your planned improvements. It also involves consideration of the **type of activity** you are training for and often your **role within the activity**. After considering these points, you are better placed to set **realistic training goals**.

There are two different approaches you can adopt in trying to improve your performance-related fitness: you can either train in the activity or train **outside** (away from) the activity.

To develop **physical fitness** you can either train through a **conditioning** approach (training through activity) or by completing a **fitness training** programme outside the activity (for example by completing a circuit- or weight-training programme). Both types of training are valid provided they follow certain principles. Relevant training methods for physical fitness programmes are explained on pages 49 and 51.

A conditioning approach to improve **skill-related fitness** needs to take place in skilful performance contexts. For example, if you wish to become fitter and more skilful at the same time, you need to ensure that you are working in demanding performance contexts. For example, a hockey player needs to ensure that any conditioned games or practices are organised to ensure that they develop skill as well as fitness. So she would consider the length of different practices (fitness) as well as the demands in different practices, e.g. level of opposition in practice (skill).

At other times you may wish to improve your skilful performance through a skill-related fitness training programme. An example of some of the exercises you could use in hockey is provided on page 52.

You are most likely to develop **mental aspects of fitness** through participation in the activity. For example, the demands of managing and controlling your emotions during a competitive game can best be met by taking part in full performance. Other relevant aspects of mental fitness such as mental rehearsal would take place just prior to a demanding performance. For example, a downhill skier will often rehearse through visualisation the best line to take on a downhill ski course.

Summary

The diagram below outlines the two models available for physical and skill-related training.

Model 1

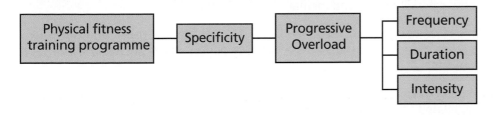

Model 2

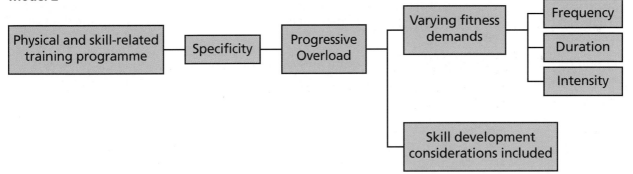

 Explain the information you would consider when setting specific performance objectives.

4 AREA 2 PREPARATION OF THE BODY

Area	Preparation of the Body
Key Concept 3	Physical, skill-related and mental aspects of fitness

In this Key Concept you **examine in detail** relevant physical, skill-related and mental aspects of fitness, how they relate to each other and how they can be applied in a training programme. You should be familiar with at least one or two aspects of physical, skill-related and mental aspects of fitness.

To be successful in an activity it is often said that 'you need the body of an athlete, the touch of a craftsman and the thought processes of a chess master'. This sums up the need for performers to possess physical, skill-related and mental aspects of fitness.

For example, to perform a backflip in gymnastics, you require **flexibility** (an aspect of physical fitness); **co-ordination** (an aspect of skill-related fitness) and **rehearsal** (an aspect of mental fitness).

As the drive is initiated, considerable flexibility is necessary in the back and shoulders of the gymnast. However, it is essential that the drive occurs at the right time in a fluent, co-ordinated way, ensuring that the knees and hips are behind the heels as the drive begins. The co-ordination of the drive is as important as the flexibility required to perform this technique.

To perform such a complex technique in a short space of time involves mentally rehearsing the series of movements that are involved. Once this has been mastered, the pattern of movements necessary can be recalled quickly from memory.

 The physical, skill-related and mental aspects of fitness are often referred to in different books by slightly different terms. Check with your teacher that the terms you are using are always accurate.

 Choose one skill or technique which requires different aspects of fitness (physical, skill-related and mental). Explain why a conditioning approach to training might be useful for the skill or technique chosen.

Aspects of Physical Fitness

Aspects of physical fitness include:

- cardiorespiratory endurance
- local muscular endurance
- strength endurance, speed endurance
- speed, strength, power (strength + speed), flexibility

The main aspects of physical fitness are:

Aspect of Fitness	Example Role and Explanation	
Cardiorespiratory endurance		**Running** This athlete has been running for a long time. She is taking a drink in order to help her run for longer. Effective cardiorespiratory endurance is the ability to transport sufficient oxygen to the working muscles during sustained exercise.
Local muscular endurance		**Rowing** The rower uses his arm and leg muscles repeatedly, over a long time. Effective local muscle endurance is the ability of working muscles.
Speed		**Sprinting** The sprinter 'drives hard' with her arms and legs to gain speed.
Strength		**Tackling in rugby** The No. 7 player needs strength to push her opponent to the ground.
Power		**Long jump** The long jumper uses speed and strength at take-off to jump a long distance.
Flexibility		**Gymnastics** The gymnast has very good hip and leg flexibility. Flexibility is the range of movement which is possible at a joint. It is affected by the type of joint and muscles attachment.

At Intermediate 2 and Higher Level, you develop further your knowledge and understanding of these aspects of physical fitness. You then need to consider how different aspects of physical fitness are often applied together for planned performance improvement in certain activities. For example, in badminton you need to develop both cardiorespiratory endurance and speed. These may initially appear as quite independent aspects of physical fitness. However, to improve both, it is often best to link them together. So, you may design a training programme that uses a general base of cardiorespiratory work with shorter bursts of speed work contained within it. This will lead to the development of '**speed endurance**'. Your training will then enable you to play long games of badminton and also enable you to cope with the particular speed demands of especially fast, intermittent bursts of play when quick court movement is required.

Strength endurance is also required in some activities. In tennis, serving involves major muscles groups working together to produce a strong service action which can be repeated, if necessary, throughout a long tennis match. This requires both muscular endurance and strength.

There are also differences within the different aspects of physical fitness. For example, within strength there is **static** strength, **explosive** strength and **dynamic** strength. Forwards in rugby try in certain scrums to hold the scrum steady. They are trying to use their static strength to prevent the other team's forwards from driving them backwards. Explosive strength is used in single actions when maximum energy is needed. Many throwing and jumping events in athletics (such as long jump and javelin) require explosive strength.

Dynamic strength is needed in swimming short distances that take up to approximately two minutes. For example, in a 100 m front crawl race, a swimmer continuously works the major muscles of the arm and shoulder to generate propulsion. In a longer race, such as the 400 m front crawl, **local muscular endurance** rather than dynamic strength would be required. Muscular endurance would be required as the performer needs to cope with the onset of **fatigue**. This will occur as waste products build up in the muscle cells as the performer tries to sustain performance over a longer period.

When planning for performance improvements in swimming, a training programme for dynamic strength would be very different from one aimed at improving muscular endurance.

Static strength

Dynamic strength
Fast swimming for a shorter time

Explosive strength

Muscular endurance
Mid-pace swimming for longer time

 Explain two aspects of physical fitness which are most required for the activities in your course.

Aspects of skill-related fitness

Aspects of skill-related fitness include:

- **agility**
- **reaction time**
- **balance**
- **timing**
- **co-ordination**
- **movement anticipation**

These aspects of skill-related fitness have an important part to play in the preparation of the body for any activity as they enable skills to be performed successfully. They can all be improved through training.

It is important that you understand these aspects without confusing them with *Skills and Techniques*, especially when answering Analysis and Development of Performance questions. (Study page 6 and check this with your teacher for further clarification.)

Agility

Agility is the ability to move the body quickly and precisely. When dribbling in hockey, you need to be able to run fast and adjust your body shape to maintain control of the stick and the ball. In hockey, agility requires both flexibility and speed.

Reaction time

Reaction time is the time taken between the recognition of a signal and the start of the movement. It is linked to speed. If you are playing as a guard in basketball you might need to move quickly to double up on marking a player cutting to the basket. A fast reaction time allied to quick court movement would assist in improving performance.

From this example you would expect that if you improve your reaction time by fitness training, your performance will improve. Remember, however, that in terms of *Skills and Techniques* the measurement of your ability as a guard would also involve other considerations, such as how well you played as part of a unit during a game.

Balance

Balance is the ability to retain the centre of gravity over your base of support. Balancing requires the control of different groups of muscles. The exact muscle requirements depend upon the nature of the task. Static balances such as a headstand in gymnastics require you to hold a balance, while dynamic balances require you to maintain balance under constantly changing conditions. When skiing you constantly adjust your dynamic balance as you travel over changing terrain in order to remain in balance.

Timing

Timing is the ability to perform skills at exactly the **right time** and with the **right degree of emphasis**.

In volleyball it is important that a player coming in to block at the net times his jump correctly so that he can block an attacking spike from the opposing team.

When driving in golf it is important that the right degree of emphasis is established. This will ensure that power will be used in conjunction with timing for maximum distance. Trying only to hit the ball very hard is rarely effective. Combining timing (through an effective well-paced swing) with power is far more likely to be successful.

Co-ordination

Co-ordination is the ability to control movements smoothly and fluently. To perform in a co-ordinated way, groups of muscles work in a specific sequence to create effective movements. For example, you need strong arm, shoulder, abdominal and back muscles to throw the javelin. However, in addition to explosive strength you require co-ordination so that your explosive strength is used at the correct stage of the throw and to its maximum potential.

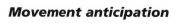

Movement anticipation

Movement anticipation is the ability to predict accurately the next set of movements that you need to make. The ability to do this is part of the detail necessary in body preparation.

In badminton you require movement anticipation to respond and move quickly to where your next shot is going to be played. To do this you need to watch your opponent carefully and anticipate as early as possible where the next shot is going and then move accordingly. For example, practising movement anticipation in badminton helps you to anticipate, by watching your opponent's movements, the difference between your opponent playing an overhead clear to the back of the court or an overhead drop shot to the front of the court. See the diagram below.

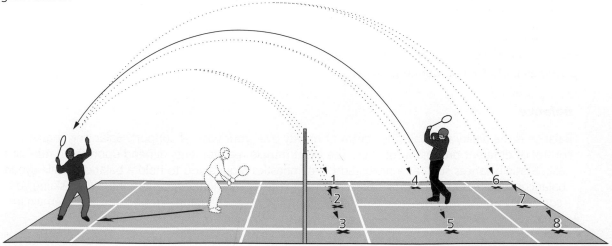

 Explain two aspects of skill-related fitness which are most required for the activities in your course.

Aspects of Mental Fitness

Aspects of mental fitness include:

- ○ level of arousal
- ○ rehearsal
- ○ managing emotions

Your level of arousal

Your level of arousal affects how well you perform. Your level of arousal needs to be just right to perform well. On occasions you may not be very interested in active participation. You may be fatigued or have other things on your mind. At these times your low level of arousal is likely to lead to your performance level being low. At other times you may be anxious or stressed because of the expectations on you to perform well. At these times your high level of arousal during performance can limit your performance.

The chart of the **Inverted U theory of arousal,** right, explains the link between your level of arousal and your level of performance.

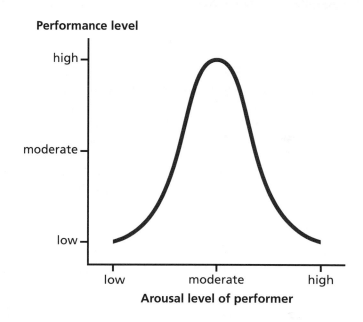

Performance level

Arousal level of performer

Rehearsal

Rehersal is the running through in your mind what you need to do to perform well prior to your actual performance. This tends to be used most in activities where you have some control of the speed and pace of your movements. For example, you can rehearse all the component parts of your golf swing prior to playing a shot. It is more difficult to do this for the return of a badminton serve. This is because your own movements are dictated by your opponent who decides which type of serve to use.

Managing your emotions

Managing your emotions is controlling your feelings in demanding situations. For example, if you are taking a penalty in football there are considerable pressures on you to score. You need to focus on what you are going to do, be positive about taking the penalty and not become easily distracted. Becoming over-anxious about taking the kick can result in a poorly taken penalty.

Managing emotions is also important when you perform in a team or group. For example, it is important to keep your shape as part of a unit. You need to listen to others and be ready to work as part of a team/group. This requires constant discipline throughout the game.

 Explain two aspects of mental fitness which are most required for the activities in your course.

4

AREA 2
PREPARATION
OF THE BODY

Area	Preparation of the Body
Key Concept 4	Principles and methods of training

In this Key Concept you **examine in detail** relevant principles of training (specificity, progressive overload, reversibility) and select an appropriate method of training to develop fitness (physical, skill-related, mental).

Principles of Training

For a training programme to be effective you need to apply these training principles to your performance:

- specificity
- progressive overload
- reversibility

Specificity

is the first key principle in training. Specificity is crucial to performance improvement: training has to be specific to your needs; it has to be relevant to the activity and to your levels of fitness and ability.

A summary of two different models to use to ensure your training is specific is outlined on page 39. For example, Model 1 could be for a swimmer who specialises in sprint events doing some land-based weight training which is designed to develop strength. Another example is a swimmer who specialises in longer distance swimming events using a land-based continuous running programme in order to develop his cardiorespiratory endurance through improving his aerobic capacity.

Model 2 is an example of a conditioning programme, for example a swimmer using a pool-based programme in order to develop the overall quality of her stroke production as well as her fitness for swimming.

Both forms of training are effective provided each programme is specific to the performer's needs and the demands of the activity.

Progressive overload

is the second key principle in training. Progressive overload is also crucial to performance improvement.

Progressive overload occurs when you exercise at increasingly greater levels: you progressively add to the demands of your fitness programme as your body adjusts to the benefits of your current fitness programme. For example, if you are an athlete training for the 5000 m, you could set time targets for all the parts of your training programme. Once you have achieved these time targets, you could create new time targets to ensure progressive overload is included in your training.

If you are a basketball player taking part in a strength training programme to improve your thigh strength, progressively increasing the weights is one way of ensuring that progressive overload is built into your programme.

In a conditioning programme for football, you could progressively overload by reducing the number of touches that you take on the ball in a small-size game. This would make you move more quickly and more often in order to retain possession. This would improve:

- your control and ability to create space
- your speed during shorter training intervals
- your cardiorespiratory endurance over longer training intervals.

The progressive overload principle can be **adapted** by varying the **frequency**, the **intensity** and the **duration** of your training.

Frequency

refers to the regularity and routine of your training sessions. How often you train varies according to the demands of the activity. Some activities require many training sessions per week over a number of months before improvements occur. For the average performer to improve cardiorespiratory endurance, he/she would need to exercise with his/her heart rate within the training zone for 20 to 30 minutes for three to four sessions per week over two to three months. However, if you are an elite performer training for competitive long distance swimming races, you would swim much more often per week. If you are a young performer in the early stages of playing full games of hockey, fitness improvements would require less training.

Intensity

refers to the relative demands of your training sessions. The intensity of your training varies according to the demands of the activity. For cardiorespiratory endurance work, you need to monitor your heart rate to ensure that you work within your training zone. Intensity can be determined by monitoring heart rate.

For sprint work involving anaerobic fitness, you need to train at a high level of intensity for shorter periods. During this anaerobic type of training, you will develop the capacity to cope with the build-up of lactic acid, which is produced by the body as a consequence of using anaerobic respiration to provide energy. This level of work can only be sustained for a short period. After a while, oxygen debt will lead to a high level of lactic acid build-up with the result that your muscles will tire and begin to work less effectively. For this reason lactate tolerance training programmes are completed by performers in many activities.

Intensity can be added to by working at a higher level of intensity. For example, a series of sprints carried out at your full 100% speed as a build-up from repetitions where you were sprinting at 80% of your maximum. The setting of the levels of intensity is very important, especially in speed/strength/power training.

Intensity can also be adapted by adjusting the work/rest interval. For example, in a cardiorespiratory endurance programme, progressively reducing the rest intervals throughout the programme adds to the intensity of the workload (even if the actual demands of the exercises remain the same).

Duration

refers to the length of planned time spent training. The duration of your training varies according to the demands of the activity. Within the context of a training programme short, intensive training sessions promote anaerobic fitness improvement; longer, moderately intensive sessions develop aerobic endurance.

Anaerobic fitness improvements are most likely to occur after six to eight weeks, provided the intensity of training work is high. Aerobic endurance improvements are most likely to occur after two to three months if the frequency of training is three to four times per week.

Duration also applies to the length of individual training sessions within a training programme (e.g. 60 minutes at the beginning rising to 80 minutes by the end of the training programme).

 Explain how you applied progressive overload within a training programme you have completed.

The dangers of over training

With any training programme it is important that you do not over train. This can be avoided by taking an adequate **rest and recovery** time during training sessions and by **avoiding over training** each week.

Consider a swimmer, specialising in sprint events, who completes a 50 m sprint and then rests for 30 seconds, before completing two further 50 m sprints with a further 30 seconds rest and recovery each time after each sprint. Following this 'set' it would be necessary to rest for 5 minutes before a further sprint set was completed. This is because it is necessary for the pulse to return to a resting level between sets to avoid over exertion. It also helps prevent any unnecessary muscle soreness created through overstretching muscles which had become unnecessarily fatigued. Taking an adequate rest and recovery is often underestimated. You should, therefore, ensure that you exercise care when deciding upon your own rest and recovery times.

Over training can be avoided by adapting the levels of frequency, intensity and duration within your training. Any of these three factors could result in over training. Regularly reviewing and monitoring your performance and completing a training diary, which records your thoughts about the effectiveness of your training, should be helpful in identifying which (if any) of these three factors could best be adapted to reduce the effects of over training.

Reversibility

If you stop training then your body will revert to the condition it was in before you began training. The time this takes to occur will be dependent upon how long you trained for. If your training has been short and only over a few weeks then the training benefits will only last for a few weeks before reversibility occurs. For training which takes place over many months the training benefits last for a longer period. This is because fitness adaptation takes a long time to establish. Once it has been established it takes a longer time before regression occurs.

Methods of Training

For your training to be effective you also need to link the principles of training (covered on pages 46 and 47) to appropriate methods of training.

Physical fitness training methods

The most important methods of training for physical fitness are: continuous training, fartlek training, circuit training, weight training and interval fitness training. These methods are described in detail on the following pages.

Continuous training

Includes

- any exercises (e.g. running, swimming and cycling) that ensure that the heart rate is operating in your training zone for approximately 20 to 30 minutes for three to four sessions per week

Venue

- indoor, outdoor or pool-based

Benefits

- develops cardiorespiratory endurance
- develops aerobic capacity
- straightforward to plan
- progressive overload achieved by exercising more often (increasing frequency), by exercising faster (increasing intensity), or by training for longer (increasing duration)

Fartlek training

Includes

- continuous running or swimming with short sprint bursts followed by a slower recovery and then more continuous paced running or swimming

Venue

- indoor, outdoor or pool-based

Benefits

- develops aerobic fitness (e.g. by continuous running) linked to training zone requirements; develops anaerobic fitness (e.g. by short, speed-endurance sprints)
- can be varied to suit your own requirements; can be adapted to terrain (e.g. using short hills for speed endurance sprints during a longer aerobic run)
- progressive overload achieved by exercising more often (frequency), by exercising faster (intensity) or by exercising for longer (duration)

Circuit training

Includes

- fixed circuit of set tasks or individual circuit based on individual's requirements
- multi-station circuit. Stations could include specific or general exercises (e.g. bench jumps, squat thrusts and sit ups)
- general exercises alternating between different major muscle areas
- planned circuit focusing on specific fitness development

Venue

- indoor: general purpose hall with minimum of equipment, mats and benches
- outdoor: open area, possibly with some specific equipment (e.g. rugby balls)

Benefits

- develops both general and specific fitness
- exercises can be adapted to suit fitness factors, e.g.
- Bench Jumps – Single bench 30 steps × 5 minutes (develops general cardiorespiratory endurance)

  or Bench Jumps – Double bench 20 steps × 3 minutes (develops specific strength)

  In this example of circuit training to develop the thigh muscles, progressive overload can be achieved by decreasing rest intervals or by increasing repetitions of exercises. Results of times taken or of number of repetitions can be recorded easily.

Weight training

Includes

- isotonic exercises in which you move the weight through the range of movement required. In a shoulder press you move from a short bent arm start to a fully straight arm out finish. Useful for developing dynamic strength.
- isometric exercises in which you hold and resist against the weight. Isometric exercises are less common than isotonic. They are useful on occasion for developing static strength. One example is holding a press-up position close to the ground for a number of seconds, and so resisting against your own body weight.
- free-standing weights and weight machines can be used for both isotonic and isometric exercises

Venue

- indoor: weight machines tend to be located in specially designed fitness suites; free-standing weights can often be used in a gymnasium or practice hall

Benefits

- develops both general and specific muscles
- develops muscular endurance as well as strength and power
- straightforward to calculate personal values for exercises (e.g. 40% to 50% of your maximum single lift if based on sets and repetitions for muscular endurance)

  In a general muscular endurance exercise, values for a shoulder press could be 2 sets of 20 repetitions at 25 kg. The same exercise could use values of 1 set of 15 repetitions at 45 kg if it was being used as a part of a strength- or power-based circuit. This figure could be calculated on 80% of a maximum single lift.

- progressive overload achieved by increasing weight (intensity) or by increasing repetition (frequency)

Interval fitness training

Includes

- any form of exercise that allows a work/rest interval to be easily calculated (e.g. swimming, provided that you can swim reasonably well). It is important that the exercises you choose are not ones that you find technically difficult. If they are, your technical limitations will make fitness improvement and measurement difficult.

Venue

- indoor, outdoor or pool-based

Benefits

- enables high intensity work to be undertaken with limited fatigue occurring. For example, a running training programme for the 1500 m could use 4 × 400 m repetitions, completed in 60 seconds with 90 seconds recovery. This causes less fatigue than a single 1500 m run. Running times could be worked out using the same percentage figures used in the weight training example: cardiorespiratory endurance work involving longer distances would be based on 40% to 50% of fastest time; speed work on 80% of fastest time.

- develops both aerobic and anaerobic capacity

- progressive overload achieved by carrying out the programme more often (frequency), by working faster or by decreasing rest intervals (intensity) or by exercising for longer (duration)

Flexibility training

Includes

- forms of flexibility or mobility exercises which allow active or passing stretching or resistance. It is important that the exercises you choose are not ones that you find technically difficult and that you exercise within a range of movement which you can manage. Avoid over stretching.

Venue

- usually indoor or outdoor

Benefits

- enables exercises to be completed which are designed to increase a range of movement around a joint. Practice at moving slowly into exercises and holding the end position for 5 seconds adds to the benefit of each exercise. The practice of stretching and then actively contracting muscles at the end of a mobility exercise enable stretching which is greater and less painful to develop.

- increase a range of movement around a joint

- progressive overload achieved by carrying out the programme more often (frequency), by working at more advanced and demanding stretching exercises (intensity) or by exercising for longer (duration).

 Choose two different physical aspects of fitness (cardiorespiratory endurance, local muscular endurance, strength endurance, speed endurance, strength, speed, power, flexibility). Explain which forms of training would be most effective to use for improving the two physical aspects of fitness chosen.

Skill-related Fitness Training Methods

For skill-related fitness the methods of training selected need to add skill demands to physical fitness demands. In many activities, players in training move around the playing area completing different tasks at each station. This is similar to circuit training for physical fitness, except that in this circuit you are completing skill-related tasks at each station.

Hockey example

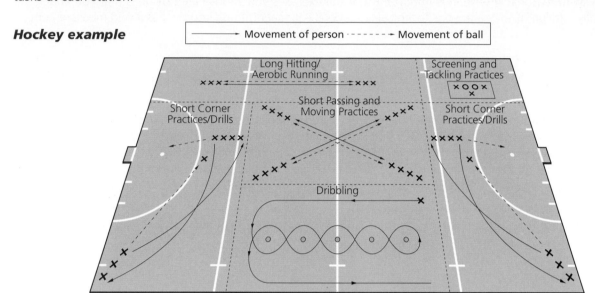

In this hockey example, the aerobic running exercise would be beneficial for improve **timing** as this is important in long hitting. The screening and tackling practices would be beneficial for improving reaction time and **movement anticipation**. This is because setting screens requires movement anticipation. The dribbling practice is useful for improving **agility** as both speed and **co-ordination** is required in this practice. The short corner practice requires quick **reaction times**. This is particularly important when the short corner is stopped and the attacking shot has to take place as soon as possible after this, so that the opposing defenders do not get too close to where the shot is taken from. **Balance** is important in the short passing and moving practice, where it is important to stay in dynamic balance when passing, moving and turning.

Choose two different skill-related aspects of fitness (reaction time, agility, movement anticipation, co-ordination, balance, timing). Explain which forms of training would be most effective to use for improving the two skill-related aspects of fitness chosen.

Mental Fitness Training Methods

Mental practice before performance can help you to manage your emotions better during performance. There are many different approaches used in this area. They often differ depending upon the nature of the activity.

The main components of mental practice are:

- selecting a quiet area, away from the competition/performance space
- establishing a clear picture in your mind of a quality performance
- breaking the performance into manageable parts
- being positive, imagining doing well

Choose two different mental aspects of fitness (concentration, focus and mental rehearsal). Explain which forms of training would be most effective to use for improving the two mental aspects of fitness chosen.

Area	Preparation of the Body
Key Concept 5	Planning, implementing and monitoring training in pursuit of personal goals

In this Key Concept you **examine in detail** phases of training or training cycles and their relationship to performance development and the importance of planning and monitoring progress in pursuit of your personal goals.

You will often plan and implement a personalised training programme in order to improve your performance. This training programme will usually be progressive in order to bring about continuous improvements. Many performers structure their long-term planning through **periodisation**.

The requirements of a training programme depend upon the **nature** of the activity: some sports, such as athletics, have a very high intensity and relatively short competitive season; in contrast, many team games such as hockey and football have long competitive seasons that last many months.

The requirements of a training programme also depend upon **your role** within an activity. In rugby union, for example, the physical fitness needs of a prop forward are different from those of a winger. Even within the same aspect of fitness an individual's personal fitness needs may be different. For example, a prop forward may need to develop greater upper body strength specifically for use in rucks and mauls; a winger may need to develop more general strength to help improve her sprinting speed.

Phases of Training

A periodised training year can be broken down into these three main **phases of training**:

- **preparation period**
- **competition period**
- **transition period**

Preparation period

includes pre-season training. **General** training is normally used at the beginning of this period. This is followed by **specific** training when there will be an increase in the intensity of physical fitness work. This could be through more demanding aerobic work or through an increase in the strength requirements of exercises within a weight- or circuit-training programme. The fitness work at this stage will be **specific** to the **nature** of the activity and **your role** within an activity, and so it concentrates on skill-related as well as physical aspects of fitness.

Competition period

During the competition period you maintain your physical and skill-related fitness. Your aim is to ensure that you can benefit from your pre-season training during full performance. Within the competitive period there may be particular competitions of special importance to you. You will want to '**peak**' for these competitions. This is easier to achieve in individual activities (such as athletics) than in team activities. In peaking for a special performance you fine-tune your preparation with a special event or competition in mind. Part of your preparation will involve a period of '**tapering down**' your training prior to competition in order to avoid any training fatigue. Following your special event or competition you will need a brief recovery time before continuing with your training.

4 AREA 2 PREPARATION OF THE BODY

Transition period

Following the competitive season you need a period of 'active rest' (the transition period). This period marks the divide between the end of one season and the start of a new preparation period for a new season. During this period it is important there is a definite break from competitive activity. However, it is also important to retain a level of **general** physical fitness during this time.

Two examples of a periodised training year, one for an athlete and one for a rugby union player are shown below.

Example 1 – A Rugby Player (winter competition)

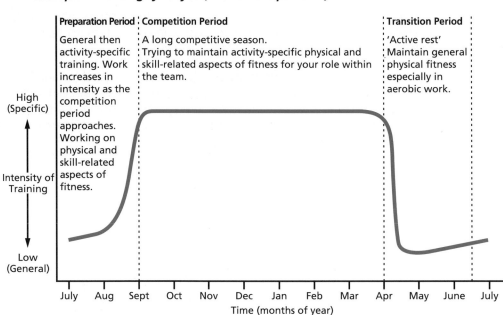

Preparation Period
General then activity-specific training. Work increases in intensity as the competition period approaches. Working on physical and skill-related aspects of fitness.

Competition Period
A long competitive season.
Trying to maintain activity-specific physical and skill-related aspects of fitness for your role within the team.

Transition Period
'Active rest'
Maintain general physical fitness especially in aerobic work.

Example 2 – An Athlete (summer competition)

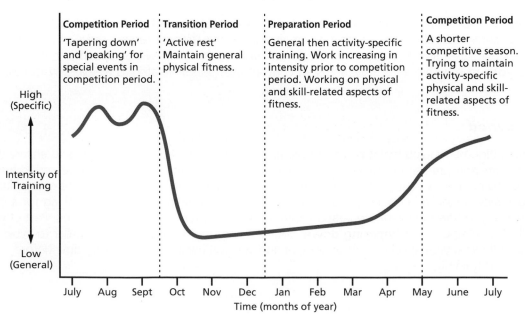

Competition Period
'Tapering down' and 'peaking' for special events in competition period.

Transition Period
'Active rest'
Maintain general physical fitness.

Preparation Period
General then activity-specific training. Work increasing in intensity prior to competition period. Working on physical and skill-related aspects of fitness.

Competition Period
A shorter competitive season. Trying to maintain activity-specific physical and skill-related aspects of fitness.

Training Cycles

Once you have analysed your training requirements you can then use training cycles to ensure your training is effective. In this way, you can ensure that your own training cycle matches the requirements of periodisation. The terms **microcycle**, **mesocycle** and **macrocycle** are often used to describe exactly what your training would include at particular times. You may wish to consider these terms as referring to your training needs over the short term (microcycle), the medium term (mesocycle), and the long term (macrocycle).

Microcycle

Using example 1 on page 54, consider a training cycle for a fast-running centre or winger. Her training cycle might include the following programme for a specified week within the microcycle:

Microcycle			
Day	**Training Objective**	**Content**	**Time/Intensity**
Sunday	Rest/recovery		
Monday	General endurance Skill circuit	Aerobic running Passing/kicking Small group team plays	30 minutes 45 minutes
Tuesday	Free		
Wednesday	Speed endurance Team plays	Different sprint drills Tactical considerations	30 minutes 45 minutes
Thursday	Speed training Muscular endurance circuit	Short sprint drills Circuit training	15 minutes 45 minutes
Friday	Free		
Saturday	Match day (80-minute game)		

Mesocycle

is the term used to describe your training pattern over the medium term. For the rugby player being profiled in the example above, this might include details of her training over a number of weeks (for example, during a one-month period in her preparation period within periodisation).

Macrocycle

is the term used to describe longer term training objectives. This would include details of your training plans for particular competitions and events and would allow for tapering down your training programme prior to competition and rest periods following competition.

Monitoring Performance

When planning your fitness training programme it is important to include the monitoring of your performance as your programme proceeds. To analyse your performance on an ongoing basis, use some of the methods of collecting information which are described on pages 14 to 20. This information will provide you with the required detail on your performance to plan adjustments to your programme. For example, if by reviewing your training log it was apparent that your training was not demanding enough then you could take active steps to adapt frequency, intensity and duration.

A midterm review of your training programme can often be very effective. For example, if you were completing a three-month cardiorespiratory training programme it would be useful to re-test your performance after six weeks. By doing this you would collect valuable information about your performance. You would establish whether you are likely to meet your targets for improvements and make any necessary changes to your training plans.

When monitoring your performance you should consider the methods of collecting information.

Choose an activity from your course. Explain how different aspects of fitness (physical, skill-related or mental) linked to the principles of training you used and to the methods you selected for collecting information).

Course assessment: revision questions

These revision questions are designed to help you improve your content knowledge (the wheel's hub – see pages 12–13) and to help you check how well you are progressing. Model answers are provided at the back of this book. Most questions can be answered within a few lines but some are a little more demanding and require additional reading to inform your answers.

> **Tip: Ensure your answers are about your performance in an activity from your course.**

Preparation of the Body

1. Give four benefits of fitness assessment at the beginning of a planned programme of performance improvement. (4)

2. Explain in detail one effective method of testing aerobic capacity. (2)

3. State three specific objectives for performance-related fitness in a team game. (3)

4. Describe three advantages of a conditioning approach to training. (3)

5. a. Give a concise definition and example of 'speed endurance'. (2)
   b. Give a concise definition and example of 'strength endurance'. (2)

6. Explain one advantage of managing your emotions during performance. (2)

7. The following line contrasts aerobic energy production with anaerobic energy production in different activities. For the given activities, place their numbers on the line at the places that show the degrees of aerobic and anaerobic energy demands involved.

   1 400 m sprint

   2 10 minute continuous swim

   3 A full (90 minute) football game

   4 A single volleyball spike

   5 1500 m race

   anaerobic ◄──────────────────────────────────── aerobic   (5)

8. Choose one specific aspect of fitness from each of the rows in the table below. Then explain how, when combined together, they are important in your performance in an activity. (You should be able to make many such combinations.) (6)

Physical aspects of fitness:	cardiorespiratory endurance, local muscular endurance, strength endurance, speed endurance, strength, speed, power, flexibility
Skill-related aspects of fitness:	reaction time, agility, movement anticipation, co-ordination, balance, timing
Mental aspects of fitness:	level of arousal, rehearsal, managing emotion

9. What is required for a training programme to be specific? (3)

10. Why is progressive overload required in fitness training programmes and what are the major ways of achieving it? (4)

11. What is the relationship between maximum oxygen uptake and lactic acid threshold? (2)

12. Explain three benefits of interval training. (3)

13. What is plyometric training? (2)

14. What is meant by lactate tolerance in training? (2)

15. Define 'periodisation'. (2)

16. Describe two advantages of tapering down your performance in a training programme. (2)

17. Within a training cycle based on preparation, competition and transition periods, what forms of training would be included during the preparation period? (3)

18. Complete the following paragraph using the following words available once each. (5)

taper   long   reduced   competition   activity

In a periodised training year, a period of overload is followed by a ____. This can last up to two weeks, during which time the training load is gradually ____ before ____. This takes place to ensure that the fitness benefit of training is not reduced through the onset of fatigue. The degree of taper in a training programme will be affected by the demands of the ____. For example, in athletics, a sprinter's taper will be relatively ____ whilst a long distance runner's taper might last only a few days.

5

AREA 3
SKILLS AND
TECHNIQUES

Key Concepts in Skills and Techniques

- **The concept of skill and skilled performance**

- **Skill/technique improvement through mechanical analysis or movement analysis or consideration of quality**

- **The development of skill and the refinement of technique**

Area	Skills and Techniques
Key Concept 1	The concept of skill and skilled performance

In this Key Concept you **examine in detail** what makes a skilled performance; how skills are performed through an information processing model; how skills and techniques are performed for effective, consistent performance and how model performance can be used to enhance and develop performance.

What makes a skilled performance?

The most important objective of a skilled performance is to carry out linked movements with **maximum efficiency**. A skilled performance shows these three characteristics:

(a) sequences of movements are carried out in a fluent, controlled way often with a minimum of effort

(b) correct options are selected

(c) skills and techniques are used which reflect the performer's ability and experience.

Skill is **relative** to ability. Your ability to play in defence at hockey determines the type of technique you can use efficiently and the type of options you can use successfully during game play. Your technique and options will probably be less extensive than those of an international hockey player, but more extensive than those of someone just beginning to learn the activity.

Basketball example

The performers in this example are working at Intermediate 2 and Higher Level in Performance. They need to show an effective level of fluency and control in performing skills in demanding situations. They:

- **show fluent, controlled movements**. The performers show very good ball handling and court movement skills. They adjust to the pace of the game and use changes of speed to cover and create space. They move in dynamic balance showing good posture and joint alignment. They use their court coverage skills to both defensive and attacking advantage.

- **select correct options**. In individual skills, the performers usually select options that are successful and inventive. For example, they pass using disguise to open up court space. They fake shots. They work out ways of taking on opponents at 1 v 1. In attack, they read set plays and take their cues from others. They consistently select the most likely successful option on free plays.

- **use skills which reflect experience and ability**. The performers play to their known strengths. In defence, they dominate space and control the movements of attackers. This applies to all defensive set-ups. In attack, they work out positions that allow the team's advantages to flourish. For example, they set screens effectively to help scoring and they recognise times when certain options are not viable. This has been learnt from their experience of regular game play.

Record the important skills and techniques in your activities, as in the example above.

Remember!

- Skill describes the **purpose** of linked sequences of movements.

- Technique is a **way** of executing a skill.

- Skills and techniques vary in difficulty according to their requirements, your ability and your previous experience.

- 'Preparation – Action – Recovery' is an effective way of analysing Skills and Techniques.

Processing information when learning skills

As your performance develops you are learning how to process relevant information effectively. The **information processing model** is one method you can use to consider how learning takes place. The model contains four parts that are linked together in a '**learning loop**'. The diagram below is an example of how the learning loop could be applied to a service reception in volleyball:

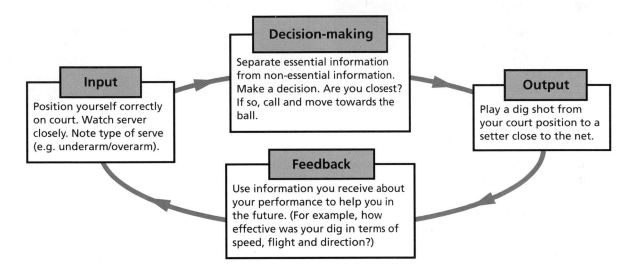

Decision-making

Separate essential information from non-essential information. Make a decision. Are you closest? If so, call and move towards the ball.

Input

Position yourself correctly on court. Watch server closely. Note type of serve (e.g. underarm/overarm).

Output

Play a dig shot from your court position to a setter close to the net.

Feedback

Use information you receive about your performance to help you in the future. (For example, how effective was your dig in terms of speed, flight and direction?)

- The first part of the loop is **input** information. This is the information you receive from your senses, e.g. sight and sound.

- You then have to make decisions based on the input information you have received. Sifting more important information from less important information is the second part of the loop – **decision-making.**

- The third part of the loop is **output**. This is the way in which you decide to move and respond to the decisions you have made.

- During and after your chosen response you will receive information about your performance. This **feedback** is the final part of the loop.

 Apply the learning loop to your own performance in an activity.

 Using the criteria of 'fluency' and 'selecting correct options' describe your level of skill in an activity from your course.

Classification of skills

Skills are predominantly closed or predominantly open, simple or complex and discrete/serial or continuous. Classifying a skill according to these different criteria is particularly helpful in determining which types of practice are most likely to improve a specific skill.

Skills exist on a continuum (a line) between closed and open: those which are unpredictable are open; those which you are in charge of carrying out are closed.

Closed ←—————————————————————————————→ **Open**

For example, in rugby no two scrums are the same. They may differ according to which team has the put-in, and whether teams are looking for a quick scrum or to hold the ball in the scrum and drive forwards. The skill of the rugby scrum is open due to its unpredictable nature.

Simple skills in gymnastics are closed. In a forward roll you follow and control simple set movements in order to carry out the technique. When the forward roll is developed into a dive forward roll, the technique is more complex to carry out. However, the demands of the technique are still closed. There are few distractions or other factors to consider when executing your performance.

Other skills have both open and closed elements. For example, the skill of driving in golf is essentially a closed one. However, applying the skill to a round of golf involves certain open demands. These might include taking into account the positioning of various hazards, bunkers, rough ground, and the strength and direction of the wind.

The classification into open and closed skills assists in understanding the learning and development of skills.

 Check whether the skills involved in the activities you are following are simple or complex. Compare your findings with those of your teacher and class colleagues.

 For the different activities in your course, classify (open-closed) the skill involved.

Skills are also either predominantly simple or complex.

Skills exist on a continuum between simple and complex: those which require little decision-making and only basic movement patterns are simple; those which require more thought and decision-making are complex.

A number of factors determine whether a skill is predominantly simple or complex. These include: the amount of information to be processed; the number of decisions to be made; the speed at which information processing and decision-making requires to occur; the accuracy involved and the amount and type of feedback which is available.

A relatively simple skill will require few of the factors mentioned above. For example, to run the 100 m sprint in a fast time requires considerable speed (physical fitness) and visualisation (mental fitness). However, the skill involved is relatively simple as it involves the straightforward repetition of a set of movements with a relatively low level of co-ordination and decision-making required.

In gymnastics a handspring vault is a complex skill. The skill is made up of many different parts (subroutines). See the diagram below for the different parts involved.

The vault requires timing in order to link the parts of the skill together effectively. For example, sufficient momentum from the take-off is needed in order to get flight onto the horse as well as off the horse. Many different sequential movements are also required in a handspring vault. The vault is also carried out at high speed, which adds further complexity to the skill.

In other athletics events such as the 1500 m middle distance run the skill demands are still relatively simple, but more complex than the shorter 100 m sprint. Complexity is added through, for example, using feedback about your performance during the race to decide on your pace judgement, making decisions about when to try to overtake other competitors and when to begin sprinting for the finish line.

lap 1   laps 2–3   lap 4

 Explain the level of complexity involved in the different skills from one activity in your course.

 Check whether the skills involved in the activities you are following are simple or complex. Compare your findings with those of your teacher and class colleagues.

Skills are also either predominantly discrete/serial or continuous.

Skills exist on a continuum between discrete/serial and continuous: those which have no clear beginning or end and are repetitious in nature are continuous skills; those which are made up of several identifiable parts are serial skills and those which have a clear beginning and end are discrete skills.

A tennis serve is an example of a discrete skill (see diagram). This skill has a clear beginning and ends as the player makes decisions about his or her court movement and future shot selection after the serve.

Serial skills are made up of a number of skills which are put together in a sequence or series. To complete a serial skill effectively you require to link the different skill movements together correctly. The javelin thrower pictured in the diagram requires to link the run up, throwing base, weight transfer and follow through together correctly for an effective throw.

Continuous skills are characterized by their ongoing nature and for having cyclical or repetitive patterns. Cycling and running are examples of continuous skills. The diagram below shows a long distance runner whose movements are continuous.

 Check whether the skills involved in the activities you are following are discrete/serial or continuous. Compare your findings with those of your teacher and class colleagues.

Comparing and contrasting your performance with a model performer is an effective way to enhance and develop performance. Pages 29 and 30 provide important details of how this process can be effectively completed.

 From one activity in your course, explain whether the skills involved are predominantly discrete, serial or continuous?

Area	Skills and Techniques
Key Concept 2	Skill/technique improvement through mechanical analysis or movement analysis or consideration of quality

In this Key Concept you **examine in detail** the purposes of collecting relevant and detailed information through mechanical and movement analysis and the consideration of quality. You then review how using information from these approaches can create a detailed plan for performance improvement and for reviewing and monitoring your performance improvement.

To plan technique improvements you can use three different types of analysis: mechanical analysis, movement analysis and consideration of quality. The type of activity you are involved in often determines which type is best. A mechanical analysis of performance is commonly used in athletics and swimming.

Mechanical analysis

In throwing events in athletics, e.g. discus, where the effectiveness of a technique can be affected by small details, a mechanical analysis may be most useful. The analysis in this example would focus on force, use of body levers and planes of movement.

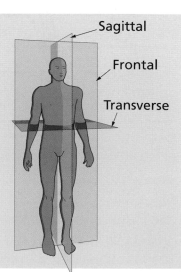

Force

The greater the force generated by turning, the greater the possibility of a long throw.

Use of body levers

The throwing arm uses a long lever. The turning force generated needs to be transferred to the throwing arm.

Planes of movement

The body can be divided into three different planes: sagittal, frontal and transverse. In the discus throw above, the athlete turns around her transverse plane to generate force.

5 AREA 3 SKILLS AND TECHNIQUES

Your specific technique requirements in other activities may mean that a mechanical analysis would be the most useful. In swimming a mechanical analysis of stroke effectiveness is often used by analysing force and resistance. Consider the diagram below.

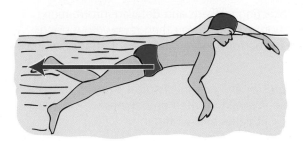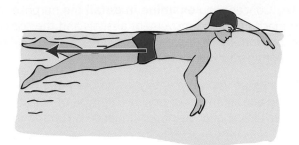

In this example, the first swimmer is having difficulty in swimming effectively due to the resistance created by poor streamlining. This is evident through the swimmer's lower centre of gravity. With the second swimmer the leg action is more effective, less water is displaced, the swimmer's centre of gravity is higher. Overall, the forces applied are overcoming the resistance created by the water in a more effective way.

Action/reaction is another method for completing a mechanical analysis of performance. This form of analysis links to Newton's Third Law of Motion. Put simply, for every action there is an equal and opposite reaction. For example, as a sprinter pushes backwards and downwards onto the blocks, there is an equal and opposite upwards and forwards reaction. Consider the swimmer in the diagram below. As they drive back against the block, there is an equal and opposite upwards and forwards reaction. As they move through the air, their weight will affect their position and entry into the water.

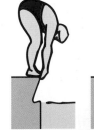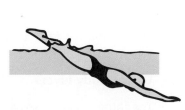

Movement analysis

In other activities a movement analysis may provide the specific technique information you require.

The observation schedule on page 15 is an example of movement analysis. It measures the effectiveness of a performer's preparation, action and recovery in playing an overhead clear shot. The criteria cover movement to play the shot, movement during the shot and movement after hitting the shuttle. This type of movement analysis is useful for analysing the effectiveness of particular techniques in many activities. By analysing in this way it is often possible to find out specific aspects of performance that require improvement. It is also useful for completing an analysis which looks at the overall effectiveness and efficiency of movements. For example, from the analysis of the overhead clear on page 15 it is evident that the player has technical difficulty with their weight transfer during the preparation and action phases. It is also evident that the court movement is ineffective through limited forward movement to mid court after completing the overhead clear follow through.

For some activities a movement analysis based on analysing effort factors is preferable to analysis of technique. When considering this form of analysis, effort factors such as weight, time, space and flow criteria are used to establish the effectiveness of performance. This method of movement analysis is common in activities such as gymnastics and dance.

Consideration of quality

In other activities consideration of quality may be the most effective way of analysing technique. The different performance qualities highlighted in *Performance Appreciation* – technical, physical, personal and special – are often used as criteria for analysis. The specific criteria selected will depend upon the demands of different activities and your role within an activity.

In association football, top strikers usually have qualities that enhance their performance: they often appear to have more time than other players; they can deceive their opponents about their intentions; they can adapt their technique to increase their effectiveness. For example, a top striker can often use little back lift in his shot preparation if necessary. When in possession he can often also keep the ball moving just prior to shooting without the need to have the ball 'set'. This adds to defenders' problems and makes their tackling and planned interceptions more difficult. In this example the qualities of time, deception and adaptation would be useful qualities to analyse.

 Explain why different methods of analysis were chosen for the different activities in your course.

Creating a plan for completing a Mechanical, Movement or Consideration of Quality Analysis

When making a detailed plan for completing an analysis of your technique you require to consider the criteria you would use for analysing the development of your performance.

Your analysis of a football tackle could, for example, focus on any of the different types of analysis outlined in the following observation schedules.

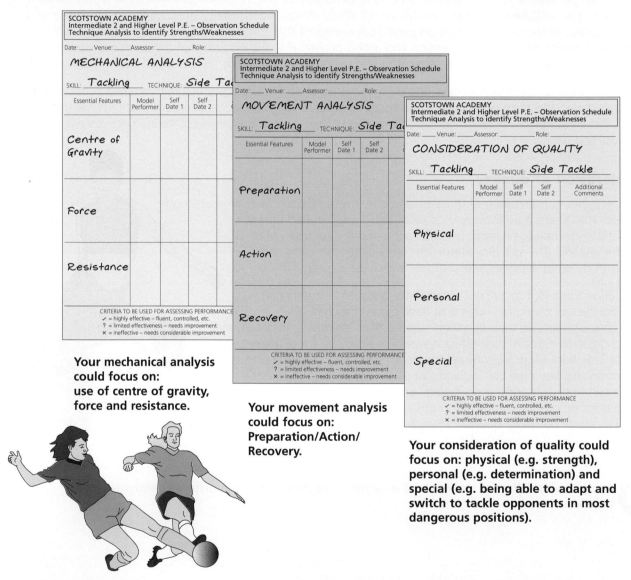

Your mechanical analysis could focus on: use of centre of gravity, force and resistance.

Your movement analysis could focus on: Preparation/Action/Recovery.

Your consideration of quality could focus on: physical (e.g. strength), personal (e.g. determination) and special (e.g. being able to adapt and switch to tackle opponents in most dangerous positions).

Collecting data in this way will provide you with valuable information. Even within specified approaches, such as movement analysis, you may consider that a different type of information is necessary to help improve your performance.

When you are completing your detailed plan for analysing technique it is important that you continually review and monitor improvements. The observation schedules on this page enable this to occur. After comparing yourself to a model performer at the outset (Self date 1) a further reassessment is possible (Self date 2) so that review and monitoring of progress is possible. Further review of progress opportunities could be added as necessary. Monitoring ongoing analysis of performance improvements would be important whenever using mechanical analysis, movement analysis or consideration of quality.

Area	Skills and Techniques
Key Concept 3	The development of skill and the refinement of technique

In this Key Concept you **examine in detail** the different stages of skill learning, principles of effective practice and methods of practice, and influential factors in the development of performance (motivation, concentration and feedback).

This Key Concept includes:

- stages of learning
- practice methods
- principles of effective practice
- motivation, concentration and feedback

Stages of Learning

When you have worked out the demands of the skills involved in an activity and checked your level of practical experience in the activity, you are in a good position to learn and develop these skills.

There are **three important stages** in learning and developing skills: the Preparation (Cognitive) Stage, the Practice (Associative) Stage and the Automatic (Autonomous) Stage.

Preparation Stage

During the preparation stage, you find out what the skill involves. You establish what the parts of the skill are and make your first attempts at learning each part. These parts of the skill are often referred to as **subroutines**. Even though the techniques used within the skill are new, it may not mean that you are at the beginner level (e.g. in gymnastics, a demanding tumbling skill may be new to you even though you are a high level performer). At this stage in learning, errors are likely to be common and so you will need advice, encouragement, and support to prevent unnecessary accidents.

Practice Stage

During the practice stage you **link together** all the required subroutines of the skill. Your ability, experience and the types of skill involved will determine the amount of practice time required. Simple skills will require less consolidation through practice than complex skills. Gradually, appropriate practice will reduce the number of mistakes made during performance.

The type of practice method you would use for the development of simple closed skills is likely to be different from those you use for complex open skills.

Automatic Stage

At the automatic stage, most key subroutines have become automatic in the performance. As a result, little attention is paid to them. During a dig in volleyball this may mean that you can move to the ball in balance, align the arms correctly and lower your centre of gravity automatically. This allows you to pay much closer attention to the flight path of the ball without devoting any special attention to the subroutines.

At the automatic stage errors are less likely. Due to your higher skill level you will be able to devote more attention to more detailed aspects of your performance. For example, in your volleyball dig you are now able to concentrate on the speed of the dig to your setter as well as on the direction and flight path of the shot.

 Choose one skill from one activity in your course. Explain whether the skill is at the preparation, practice or automatic stage. Justify your choice with examples from your performance.

5

AREA 3
SKILLS AND
TECHNIQUES

Practice Methods

When developing skills and techniques you use different methods of practice. The most common methods are:

- Solo/shadow/partner/group
- Opposed/unopposed
- Gradual build-up
- Repetition/drills practices
- Massed/distributed
- Conditioned games/small-sided games/coached games
- Whole/part/whole

Solo/shadow/partner/group

These various forms of practice are useful for ensuring that the demands of different practices are specific and allow performance progression. This helps ensure practices are **realistic**. For example:

practising skills under a time restriction

having to score a certain amount in a limited time.

For example, imagine you are involved in the following court movement practice in badminton. See diagram 1. The aim of this practice is to move from the start, through positions X1 to X4 returning to the finish position. During this short practice you will need to change direction, stay in balance when moving, use precise footwork and cover the court in a fast, effective way.

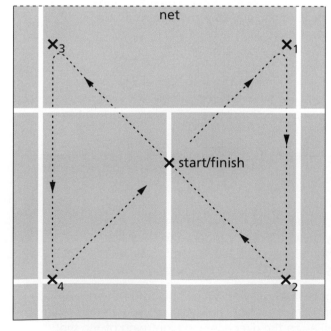

Diagram 1

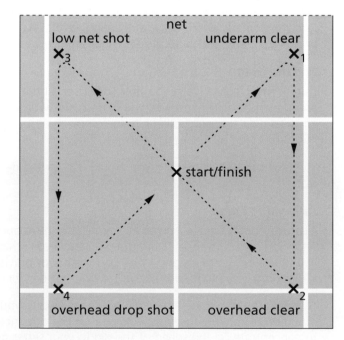

Diagram 2

This can be practised, firstly, as a **solo** practice. This will help you establish the pattern and routine of the practice. It will help establish the many changes of direction and body position required. At this time you will be under no time pressure or required to shadow another player.

One way of adding progression to this practice would be to **shadow** (mirror) another badminton player completing the same court movement routine. This would require you to focus on the movements of the other player at the same time as you were focusing on your own court movement. In badminton, trying to watch the court movement and positioning of your opponent at all times is an important performance quality to develop. This would be a useful practice development, because as your skill ability level improves so must the demands of practices.

One advantage of this varied form of practice is that **training intervals** can be included. You may be required to complete the movement practice using a training interval that takes into account your existing skill and fitness levels in badminton. You could then be matched with a **partner** of similar abilities to add variations to the practice. For example, you might shadow your partner as previously, but on this occasion your partner can call for a change in direction at any time. This requires you to react quickly and be alert. In this type of practice your partner could work co-operatively with you. If you were to fall too far behind your partner would slow to allow you to catch up, so that the practice was meaningful.

 If the practice outlined in diagram 1 is used as a starting practice, further progression can be added to it to make it increasingly demanding. You could simulate different shots as you move towards each of the court corners before returning again to the court centre. When at corner X1 you could play an underarm clear before moving backwards to play an overhead clear from corner X2; you could then move diagonally forwards to play a low net shot from position X3 before moving backwards again to play an overhead drop shot from position X4. (See diagram 2.) You could then complete this practice against a set time and work to reduce this time as you improve.

Many varieties of shot selection and patterns of movement could also be added to this simple practice set-up. Further progression could then be added by, for example, others in your **group** positioning themselves at each of the four court corners, with a shuttlecock each. As you move to each corner, with good footwork and balance and your racket ready, the colleague there could feed a shuttlecock to you so that you could play each of the four shots previously described. Where your shots land would provide useful information about your shot effectiveness under pressure. This could be carried out on a 10-second work time to complete practice followed by 40-second recovery time, as you and the four others in your group rotate around the different position in the practice.

 Explain when you have used solo/shadow/partner/group practices on your course.

5

AREA 3
SKILLS AND
TECHNIQUES

Opposed/unopposed

Varying the degree of opposition is a useful way of making practice meaningful and of avoiding practice which is inappropriate. Study the diagram below, which involves three different lay-up practices in basketball. The three practices are characterised by having no opposition, passive (limited) opposition and active (full) opposition. Completing the practice with no opposition can be useful at the preparation stage of skill learning. Practising with limited opposition would suit skill learning at the practice stage. Practice with active opposition would suit skill learning at the automatic stage. When working with passive and active levels of opposition, it is important that your partner is aware of the level of opposition they are expected to provide. This will ensure that the benefits of practice are maximised.

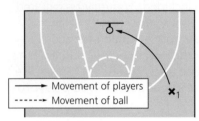

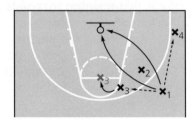

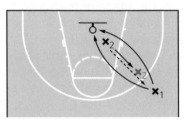

Practice description

Player X_1 dribbles towards the basket in a curved approach, jumps up and releases the ball onto the backboard.

Opposition none

Target
- controlled dribbling
- jump up off one foot with ball held securely
- release ball softly onto backboard
- land on two feet in balance
- score a basket occasionally

Practice description

Player X_1 passes to either player X_3 or X_4. She then cuts to the basket and receives a pass back from either X_3 or X_4. X_2 provides some opposition as a defender as player X_1 dribbles towards the basket, jumps high and attempts to score.

Opposition passive

Target
- cut to the correct side (e.g. if pass is to X_4, then cut between X_4 and X_2)
- control the ball when dribbling
- shield the ball from the defender
- jump high in balance
- score a basket regularly

Practice description

Player X_2 passes the ball out to player X_1 and then runs out to defend against player X_1. Player X_1 has to cut and drive past defender X_2 in order to get close to the basket and complete a lay-up shot.

Opposition active

Target
- cut and drive quickly and forcefully to the basket
- shield the ball
- jump high in balance
- score a basket often

Gradual build-up

This is a useful practice method for learning **complex** skills. It is also a useful method if the skill involves an element of **risk**. By using gradual build-up, you can make the practice more demanding in small instalments. This way of practising also allows you to develop high levels of confidence. For example, complicated sequences in trampolining can be developed **in stages**. This is achieved by gradually increasing the demands of the practice (e.g. by practising longer sequences of a trampolining routine or by practising more difficult combinations within the routine or by a combination of both).

It is essential when using gradual build-up that all practices are geared to the correct stage in your learning. Practices should be challenging yet **achievable**. They should be geared to your level of performance in order to be meaningful and realistic.

Gradual build-up practices can also be used to develop specific aspects of play during games. For example, a basketball training set-up could involve a cross-court 2 v 2 practice with passive opposition and no dribbling. Organising the practice in this way controls the demands of the practice.

Consider how this basketball practice could be built up in a gradual way to become more demanding. Consider the following variables: reference to the court area used; number of players involved; the skills allowed during the practice; the degree of opposition against which the skills are to be developed.

Explain why gradual build-up is a useful method for complex skills.

Repetition/drills practices

Repetition

During practice it can be productive to set up training drills that repeat particular parts of a technique or the whole technique itself. You may practise very small parts of the technique repeatedly. The intention is to groove the technique so that all the components of it work well together. Top performers in tennis often practise parts of a technique on its own, e.g. the toss-up of the ball in the service action. The intention is to introduce an improved part of the technique into the whole service action later. (Practising your golf swing is another example.)

This type of attention to detail works best with **complex, closed skills**.

Drills

Drills can work well when both repetition and different degrees of pressure are involved.

Badminton players often practice simple repetitive drills. In this example (see diagram 3), players work co-operatively in a demanding practice. They dictate the pressure demands of the practice by the way in which they execute the shots. If, on shot 3, the overhead clear return is played right to the back of the court, the overhead drop shot return on shot 4 will be more demanding to play. In turn, if shot 4 is played very close to the net, the first shot (shot 1) of the new cycle will be more demanding. In such a practice the aim is to keep the cycle of shots played continuously for as long as possible. If any errors occur, you would stop and restart with shot 1. This is preferable to carrying on with broken, uncertain and unstructured practice.

Diagram 3: Badminton Drills

These drills are useful for the development of court movement skills and for playing different shots under pressure. Variations can be built into them. For example, a skilled pair of badminton players could agree to change the shots played after three successful cycles of the practice. This could be achieved by playing a low return to the front of the court on shot 2 rather than a high clear to the back of the court. Then a high clear could be played to set the cycle in motion again. So the two shots played can be reversed to give practice of different shots under pressure. This would improve the quality and relevance of the practice.

5

AREA 3
SKILLS AND
TECHNIQUES

Massed/distributed

The demands of different activities influence whether practising different skills and techniques would best be practised on a **massed** (continuous) basis or by **distributed** (spaced) practice basis.

In deciding which form of practice is best, the demand of the skills (simple versus complex), the ability level of the performer, the performer's level of motivation and whether practising under fatiguing conditions is worthwhile or not, require to be considered.

For example, in orienteering, the running skill demands are relatively straightforward and practising when tired and fatigued is important. The essence of effective orienteering is to make good map reading decisions when tired, as the event is physically and mentally demanding. A continuous massed practice would benefit you as it would make the practice challenges close to those experienced when competing in orienteering competitions.

Distributed short practice would be best if you were completing a complex technique which lasted a short amount of time, for example, a backflip in gymnastics (see photograph). In this technique, there is a danger of injury if you become too tired. Therefore, a short number of practice attempts interspersed with longer rest intervals would be best. During rest intervals mental rehearsal training could be completed in order for you to focus on the order and component parts of this complex technique.

Conditioned games/small-sided games/coached games

When you are learning and developing **open** skills, you can practise different options which reflect the demands of many types of games.

Conditioned games can take various forms. Very often conditioned games are used to provide one side with an advantage. This makes achieving tasks easier. In different directly competitive games it is often possible to have two players, for example, who play for whichever team has possession of the ball at any given time. This creates attacking advantages for the team in possession and increases the demands on defenders in their efforts to regain possession. For example, you might have a cross court game of basketball with 3 v 3 but with 2 additional players playing for the attacking team. This would make it 5 v 3 when an attack is taking place. This should open up more attacking passing options which will lead to higher percentage shots being taken and more baskets being scored. If 5 v 3 is too great an attacking advantage, then the advantage could be reduced to one additional player making it 4 v 3 when a team is attacking.

Another example could occur in hockey if a 4 v 4 game on a reduced size pitch was conditioned by adding two attackers. The increase in attacking numbers should enable your repertoire of skills, decision-making and control and fluency to improve through the extra practice opportunities provided.

Conditioned games can also involve certain adaptations to the formal rules of the game. This is designed to emphasise through the game the particular skills and techniques that you have been working on earlier. For example, in basketball, if scoring through a lay-up had been emphasised in practices then one condition possible in a game would be to increase the points awarded for a basket scored through a lay-up shot.

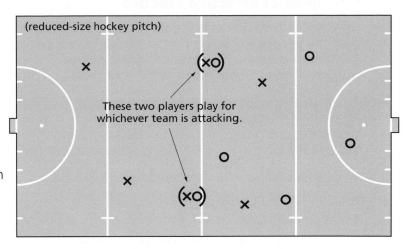

(reduced-size hockey pitch)

These two players play for whichever team is attacking.

 Consider how the different activities in your course could be adapted to improve your skills. Discuss your answer with your class colleagues and teacher.

Small-sided games such as a small 5 v 5 game of hockey can be effective as a method for improving performance. Reducing the number of players in a team provides each player with the opportunity to practise skills and techniques in game-like settings. The reduction in the number of players usually enables players to increase their level of involvement and possession of the ball. For example, if you were looking at passing, deciding when to pass, to whom to pass, the weight of the pass and the timing of the pass help you understand the demands of passing when you are making these decisions in small-sided games. The more you specifically practise this when under game-like pressure the better your performance will be, provided the demands of the small-sided games are ones which match your existing performance level.

Coached games focus on achieving specific objectives which your coach/teacher considers critical for game improvement. For example in hockey, your coach/teacher might consider that the benefits gained from practising passing under pressure require to be emphasised through the game as much as possible, so that each player in the team can see examples of improvement. For this reason the coach/teacher might have 'freeze moments' during the game to select particular examples which highlight the benefits that practice has had on game performance.

Whole/part/whole

This is commonly used by performers who already have some experience of the activity. It works best when you can perform a version of the whole skill already.

From an early analysis of the performance, any technical weaknesses can be isolated and practised as parts. Once performance weaknesses have been improved, the whole skill can then be performed again. Learning the demands of the skill will determine whether whole/part/whole is a feasible practice method. Skills which allow parts of the performance to be **separated** easily from the whole performance work best.

For example, if a performer of a basketball lay-up has a technical weakness in releasing the ball (identified in the action part of the lay-up), then jumping and practising the release of the ball on its own before returning to a basketball game could bring about performance improvement in shooting.

Whole/part/whole works less well for continuous actions. For example, it is difficult to separate parts of a handspring vault in gymnastics and practise them separately.

5 AREA 3 SKILLS AND TECHNIQUES

Principles of Effective Practice

For your practice to be effective **clear objectives** should be set. This will involve consideration of your present strengths and weaknesses and what aspects of your performance you are trying to improve. You may want to measure your current performance against a model performer. Two further important considerations are the work/rest ratio and progression within your chosen practices.

Work/rest ratio

In all forms of training you need to calculate the ratio of work relative to rest. Working out this ratio is one of the key issues in making skill training **specific** to your needs. The ratio varies according to:

- your previous experience in the activity
- your level of practical ability
- the complexity of the skill involved
- the physical demands involved in the practice.

    Always consider the training intervals of work/rest when planning your practices.

Progression

Ensure that your practices are meaningful to your current performance level and progress when you are ready to do more demanding practices. Make sure that you are working at a suitably demanding level at all times. Apply the principle of progression to all your practices. **High quality practice** for a short time is better than repetitive, low quality practice over a long time. This will ensure that your performance does not suffer from the adverse effects of boredom and fatigue.

The diagram below shows one example of how you could apply your current level of performance and stage of skill learning to designing effective practices for skill training. This example is for a basketball lay-up **opposed/unopposed** practice which has been described earlier in detail.

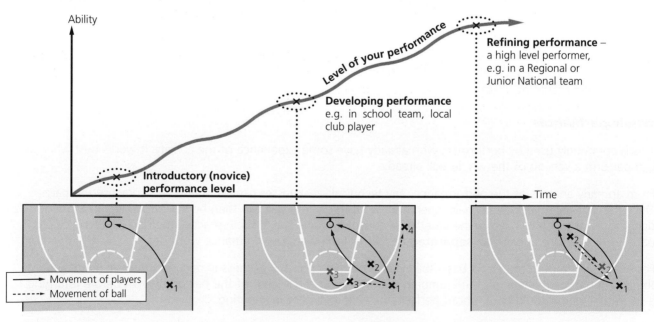

 Explain the practice objectives you have set for the different activities on your course.

Motivation, Concentration and Feedback

Once you have considered your stage of learning, methods of practice and principles of effective practice, it is useful to study how motivation, concentration and feedback affect your performance.

Motivation

Motivation is your level of desire to succeed. You need to be motivated in order to improve your level of performance. Motivation is an important factor in learning practical skills. Your aim is to optimise your motivation for the performance you are working on.

The most common distinction is whether your motivation is internal (intrinsic) or external (extrinsic).

Internal Motivation

is your own 'internal' level of desire to succeed. If you are interested and purposeful in your work, you are far more likely to make progress. If you are a talented swimmer who has to train up to eight times per week, a high level of internal motivation is essential. You need to have a high level of internal motivation as well as high levels of fitness and skill to succeed.

Your level of internal motivation will already have helped you choose your activities. There may be activities that you have sampled but chosen not to pursue. This may have arisen because your interest in them was not high enough, rather than for other reasons (e.g. the high costs involved or because none of your close friends enjoyed this activity).

External Motivation

occurs when your involvement in an activity is for reasons apart from simply participation. For example, earning money through competing is an external motivation.

Having only external motivation is rare in Physical Education and Sport. More commonly, both internal and external motivation are involved: for example, by passing Units and Course Assessments at Intermediate 2 and Higher Level Physical Education, you may wish to enjoy developing your performance level (an internal motivation) as well as using the qualification for entry into Further and Higher Education (an external motivation).

It is important to understand that your level of motivation for **different** activities may be very different from that of other colleagues. One of the reasons there are so many sports available to participate in is individuals' different motivations. You may prefer activities with **closed** skills that are not directly competitive, such as archery or gymnastics. You may enjoy the particular demands of these activities in terms of definition and attention to detail, coupled with the relative lack of outside pressure. Alternatively, you may enjoy **open**, competitive games with all the demands of performing under pressure. You may enjoy the thrill of being part of a team.

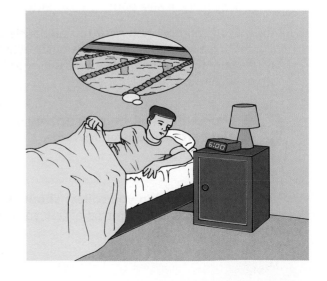

Everyone has an **optimum** level of motivation. You have probably been in situations where your fear of failure or desire to do well has adversely affected performance. Top performers become proficient at (and can develop their ability in) motivating themselves to the optimum level required for a special performance.

5

AREA 3
SKILLS AND
TECHNIQUES

Use **goal-setting** to ensure that you can perform at your highest level. Goal-setting involves you (either individually or with your teacher or coach) setting challenging **targets** which are **specific** to your performance. For example, in golf you might create a simple target of trying only to two-putt on any green. So, you would have an identifiable target for a particular part of your game. Once this has been achieved you could reset the target to two-putting every green with at least four single-putted holes.

Developing this kind of planned approach is likely to ensure that your confidence is high. You will perform better if you are able to use the knowledge and confidence gained from previous successes and incorporate them into the next practice session or competition.

 Explain the difference between internal and external motivation? Explain what optimum level of motivation means for an activity on your course?

Concentration

To perform at a high level you need to pay part attention to some cues and full attention to others. This is a major feature of performance in all activities.

When you are defending against many players during a fast break attack in basketball, you need to focus most attention on certain factors. These factors include the movement of the ball and the next player receiving the ball, until a scoring opportunity is generated. During this passage of play (which only lasts a matter of seconds), you need to select correctly which factors to pay most attention to, and which other factors are present but not essential at the time. These other factors might include the players initially involved in setting up the fast break (for example, through playing an outlet pass), who then play no further part in the attacking move.

Even in closed skills the level and focus of your concentration affects the quality of your performance. When completing a tumbling sequence in gymnastics you need to pay full attention to the quality of flight, degree of control and definition of certain techniques. You probably only need to pay part attention to other more straightforward aspects of a sequence, such as direction of travel. This is because you have managed as a high level performer to develop the ability to focus your attention on the most important parts of your sequence and partially relegate others. You have some concentration focused at a minimum level on direction. This allows you to take some corrective measures during your tumbling sequence, if necessary. However, unless it is necessary to take any corrective measures, you focus all your concentration on the key elements already identified.

If you are a beginner, you are unable to operate at this level: you need to devote all of your concentration to the more simple aspects of the sequence during the planning stage (in order to become familiar with the demands of the sequence). As your practice develops, you begin to pay selective attention to some of the more immediately manageable parts of your sequence.

Your level of concentration must be compatible with the demands of the task. In most activities you cannot pay full attention all the time. So, you heighten your level of concentration at special times so that you are alert, and pay less attention at other times. This is especially the case with activities that have a pronounced start/stop pattern of play (e.g. racquet sports).

 Choose one skill from an activity on your course. Explain the performance factors you paid full and partial attention towards.

Feedback

Feedback is **information you collect about your performance**. There are different types of feedback. The types you use depend on the type of task you are completing, the type of skill being performed and the nature of the activity.

Using feedback in a meaningful way is essential for **performance improvement**. It helps you to plan improvements to your performance and provides reinforcement about the successful parts of your performance, encouraging you to work towards further improvement.

The main types of feedback you should understand are:

Internal (Intrinsic) Feedback

concerns movement awareness (e.g. the feeling of different parts of the action)

External (Extrinsic) Feedback

includes knowledge of results, observation schedules, factors affecting results, video of performances, and information from teachers or coaches

For example, in a volleyball spike you would receive internal feedback about the action through the control, balance, co-ordination and timing you felt when completing the skill; you would receive external feedback on the same spike based on the result of the spike (e.g. a point won) and also when your teacher has given you some information about the factors that led to the successful spike.

You should use feedback in a way that relates effectively to the activity being pursued. For example, in gymnastics you could use **internal** feedback (through your body movement) to gain awareness about the qualities and actions involved in a floor routine. When completing a backward roll through handstand, you should be aware of when to push and drive upwards with your arms. As a result, you will develop a feeling and awareness of what is a good performance.

For the same action you could use various forms of **external** feedback: you could use a video of your gymnastic routine to study some of the factors that affected the performance. This could provide information about whether or not you opened out too early in your backward roll through handstand.

In competitive games, knowledge of results can be a useful form of external feedback. As the pattern and speed of play can often be quick and constantly changing, studying information about it after the performance can provide detail. In basketball, an observation schedule on your defensive rebounding in a game could detail the number of rebounds won or lost. It could then move on to provide more exact details on the level of opposition, the angle and the type of shot rebounded.

For feedback to be effective it needs to be **positive**: positive feedback focuses on what you did well and suggests how further improvements could be made. Giving negative feedback to someone is not useful as it fails to explain how improvements can take place.

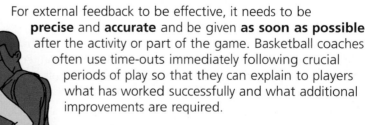

For external feedback to be effective, it needs to be **precise** and **accurate** and be given **as soon as possible** after the activity or part of the game. Basketball coaches often use time-outs immediately following crucial periods of play so that they can explain to players what has worked successfully and what additional improvements are required.

Remember that feedback and motivation are linked. You are likely to be motivated to do well in an activity if you receive positive feedback about your performance when learning and developing your skills. Positive feedback is also important when goal-setting. If your goal is to stay tighter in the tuck when completing a back somersault in trampolining, your teacher may study your performance and then give you feedback. Alternatively, you may have your performance taken on video. You could then link this analysis to your own kinaesthetic awareness (sense of your body's movement) of how your back somersault felt when you completed it. This would reward you with positive feedback about your performance and assist in sustaining and optimising your level of motivation.

Study the photograph below. The basketball player is getting internal feedback through kinaesthetic awareness of how the shot 'feels'. In addition, he is receiving external feedback through observing closely the degree of opposition when shooting.

 Give two examples of intrinsic and extrinsic feedback from one activity in your course.

Refinement of techniques

In summary, in this Key Concept, it is important for you to connect stages of learning, methods of practice, principles of effective practice and the study of motivation, concentration and feedback together effectively. Try in your skills learning to refine technique through carefully considering how these areas within the Key Concept link together.

Course assessment: revision questions

These revision questions are designed to help you improve your content knowledge (the wheel's hub – see page 11 to 13) and to help you check how well you are progressing. Model answers are provided at the back of the book. Most questions can be answered within a few lines but some are a little more demanding and require additional reading to inform your answers.

> **Tip:** Ensure your answers are about **your performance** in an activity from **your course.**

Skills and Techniques

1. Describe five qualities you would expect to see in a skilled performance.

2. Complete these sentences by using each of the following words once.

   learning decision-making output feedback input perception sequential read

   The information processing approach to ____ involves considering the importance of ____ and decision-making. This approach centres on how well you learn to ____ the information available and interpret correctly what to do in a ____ order. There are four key stages involved. These are ____, ____, ____ and ____.

3. Describe the importance of the information processing approach to learning in terms of performance learning.

4. Place the following skills along the open–closed continuum:

   1 High jump

   2 Setting in volleyball

   3 Serving in volleyball

   4 Football tackle

   5 Cartwheel in gymnastics

   5 Free throw in basketball

   Closed ←——————————————————————————→ Open

5. Provide an example and explanation of one activity that contains both open and essentially closed skills.

6. Technique improvement can be judged by mechanical analysis, movement analysis or by consideration of quality. Explain the judgements you would make when using these three methods of analysing performance.

7. Describe the importance of the relationship between stages of skill learning and principles of effective practice.

8. Describe the difference between a *simple* technique and a *complex* technique. Provide an example and explanation of each from the same activity.

9. Explain the form and uses of external feedback at each of the stages of skill learning.

10. Give an example and explanation of a particular method of practice, which would work effectively in the development of a *simple* technique.

11. Give an example and explanation of a particular method of practice, which would work effectively in the development of a *complex* technique.

12. Explain the benefits of selective attention within a specific role in a team game.

13. Explain the importance of the relationship between internal goal-setting and internal motivation.

14. When and how should positive feedback be offered to a performer?

15. Choose one activity. Explain how you organised two methods of practice, which were specific to your ability within a training programme for that activity. For each practice, explain how the practices related to your stage of skill learning and the types of feedback you received in the development of your performance.

6 AREA 4 STRUCTURES, STRATEGIES AND COMPOSITION

Key Concepts in Structures, Strategies and Composition

- The structures, strategies and/or compositional elements that are fundamental to activities

- Identification of strengths and weaknesses in performance in terms of:
  - roles and relationships, formations, tactical or design elements, choreography and composition

- Information processing, problem-solving and decision-making when working to develop and improve performance

Area	Structures, Strategies and Composition
Key Concept 1	The structures, strategies and/or compositional elements that are fundamental to activities

In this Key Concept you **examine in detail** the fundamentals of either structures and strategies or structure and compositional considerations.

Structure and strategy fundamentals are commonly used in different competitive individual and team games. These could include how to **use space** to your advantage when attacking and how to **deny space** when you are defending (for example, through applying pressure on attacking opponents). This might then lead you further into studying how to outmanoeuvre opponents when attacking and manoeuvre them to where you wish them to go when defending.

This area also studies the pattern of play you adopt when playing individual indirectly competitive activities such as badminton as well as directly competitive team games such as basketball.

In a singles game of badminton you can try to control the **tempo** of the game to suit your game plan. If the structure and strategy you decided upon when going onto court was to play an attacking game, then you would be trying to play at a fast tempo through trying to play attacking downward shots such as low returns and overhead smashes. This would help you in trying to win points in quick short rallies. If the structure and strategy you decided upon when going onto court was to play a defensive game, then you would be trying to play at a slow tempo through trying to play defensive shots such as high returns and overhead clears. This would help you in trying to win points by tiring your opponent and keeping them away from the centre of the court until a clear attacking (high percentage) opportunity occurred.

In a game of basketball, you can also try to control the tempo of the game to suit your game plan. If the structure and strategy you decided upon when going onto court was to play an attacking game, then you would be trying to play at a fast tempo through trying to attack as quickly as possible. This would involve trying to initiate 'fast break' attacks which resulted in a scoring opportunity before the defending team was properly organised.

 Give an example of tempo from one activity on your course.

Structure and composition fundamentals consider the inventive nature of performance and are commonly used in dance and gymnastics. This often involves considering design, form and style in performance. For example, in a dance performance **design** elements may include how you plan to use space creatively and effectively, and in the development of different movement motifs. **Form** includes details of how the dance is organised (e.g. through the use of different themes or through different movement patterns – rondo, canon, etc). In considering dance form you might require to consider how often you repeat certain movements, and how often contrasting movements which show variety and creativity are selected. **Style** includes categories of dance (e.g. Scottish, jazz and modern). As well as design, form and style, how you interpret different stimuli within performance requires consideration. For example, does your projection in performance reflect the stimulus which is provided by the music being used to accompany performance?

Use of space is also an important consideration within structure and composition. In gymnastics, your planning of a floor sequence will require you to consider how you will arrange your performance to best use the space available.

In the remainder of this section of the *Course Notes*, examples of the fundamentals of structure and strategy and structure and composition are highlighted and expanded upon in many different activities – football, basketball, cricket, rugby and dance.

Area	Structures, Strategies and Composition
Key Concept 2	Identification of strengths and weaknesses in performance in terms of: roles and relationships; formations; tactical or design elements; choreography and composition

In this Key Concept you **examine in detail** roles and relationships; formations; tactical and design elements; choreography and composition.

Roles and relationships

In every group or team it is essential to understand what your individual responsibilities are and how your role relates to your team-mates.

Here is an example of different players' attacking responsibilities in basketball, in order of importance:

Order of importance	Guards	Forwards	Centre
1	dribbling	shooting	rebounding
2	passing	rebounding	shooting
3	shooting	passing	passing
4	rebounding	dribbling	dribbling

Each type of player has a different role to play in order for the team to work together effectively. The success of any attacking and defending strategy depends on how well the team operates as a **unit**, with each player performing **his/her own role** to the best of their ability.

The individual role which you adopt in a group or team activity will be dependent on many factors. These may include your physical attributes and your ability as a skilled performer, including your decision-making qualities. When each individual's strengths and weaknesses are considered then a relevant structure and strategy or structure and composition can be planned.

Formations

In group or team activities you use your knowledge of your overall strengths and weaknesses as part of your planning for performance. In doing this you make decisions about the benefits and limitations of different formations within activities.

In association football, the most widely used formations are 4-4-2 and 3-5-2. The numbers refer to the number of defenders, midfield players and attackers in a team.

Recently some teams have experimented with a 3-5-2 formation with the aim of improving their performance. The main **positional** differences between a 4-4-2 and a 3-5-2 formation are: in a 4-4-2 formation you have an extra defender, as you have four players playing defence instead of three; in a 3-5-2 formation one of the defenders becomes an extra midfielder.

The strengths and weaknesses of each formation are:

4-4-2 Strengths

- Strong defensive formation with two central defenders
- Clear channels from defence to midfield

4-4-2 Weaknesses

- Limited depth in attack on occasions
- Can be difficult to get midfield players forward
- Can be caught in flat positions which affects mobility

3-5-2 Strengths

- More mobile than 4-4-2 and so easier to dominate midfield
- Can be easier to cover wide areas
- More attacking options

3-5-2 Weaknesses

- Defence can be exposed, either by width from opposition in attack, or when midfield is bypassed when longer passes are played by opposition from defence straight to attack.

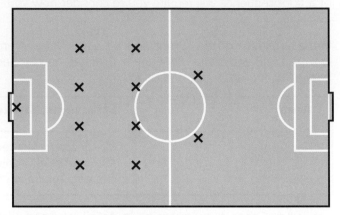

Diagram 1: a 4-4-2 formation in action

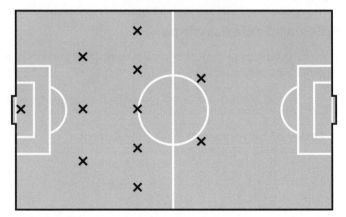

Diagram 2: a 3-5-2 formation in action

By collecting information about your team's performance, you can make decisions about which of these formations is most effective to use. You can then either continually refine your chosen formation or use another formation if your team's performance is less than you expected. Some football teams use different formations to suit their needs in particular games when playing against particular opponents.

Occasionally formations can change within the same game. This could be as the result of a coach considering that formation changes would improve team performance. It could also result from any injuries or substitutions that made formation changes desirable.

In using a chosen formation you need to analyse strengths and weaknesses. In a team formation it is useful to consider relevant principles of play. In football and basketball, for example, through considering **width**, **depth** and **mobility**. In other activities other terms are used. For example, in rugby union, formations are often analysed in terms of **support**, **continuity** and **pressure**.

A basketball example

In any area of play, a team aims to ensure that the formation(s) adopted is/are able to cover successfully the width of the playing area as well as the depth (length) of the playing area. In addition, mobility must be a feature of the formation, allowing the team to adapt and respond to either a change in team strategy or to the actions of the opposition.

Diagram 3 shows a triangular formation with one guard at the top of the key and two forwards in wide positions. If the forwards are strong at attacking 1 v 1 against their marking defenders, this set-up can be effective. If they can drive past the defenders to the basket they will show depth and mobility in their attacking moves. They will also be able to create depth and mobility if the forward without possession of the ball is able to cut to the basket and receive a pass from the forward with the ball.

However, these types of move are quite demanding to carry out. Passing directly from forward to forward is difficult as the ball needs to travel over two defenders. Passing back to the guard who then passes to the other forward is an option. However, in most situations the defending team would be quite content to let this occur. The attacking team is retaining possession of the ball, but at a long way from the basket.

These basketball examples have been developed from small-sided games. Diagrams 3 and 4 illustrate how team principles are important in a 3 v 3 game. These diagrams aim to show the importance of team principles at all levels of game play.

Diagram 4 shows a different formation that may work more effectively to create depth and mobility in attack. In this set-up there is one guard, one forward and one centre. The centre ensures that he is on the same side as the forward. This creates depth more easily as the forward and centre are closer together. If the ball can be passed to the centre then he is in a strong scoring position. The centre is also in a very good position to secure rebounds should the forward decide to take a set shot or jump shot.

These team principles continue to be important as the game progresses towards a full 5 v 5 game. Diagram 5 shows the importance of team principles within a 4 v 4 game. In this set-up, width is created by the two forwards and depth is created by the centre. The centre moves to be on the same side of the court that the ball is on. The forwards work up and down the sidelines of the court in order to retain possession and create attacking opportunities. By moving along the top of the key the guard ensures that outlet passes can be made to and between the two forwards with little risk of a pass being intercepted.

The forwards can make cuts across the key in order to make passes to another moving player (to create mobility). Defenders find this more difficult to defend against than defending against a static attacker.

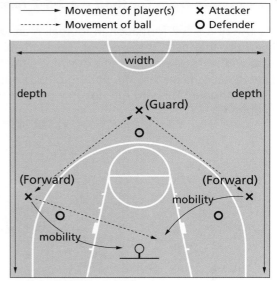

Diagram 3: a 3 v 3 game

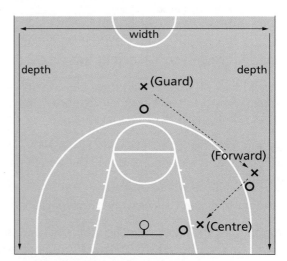

Diagram 4: another 3 v 3 game

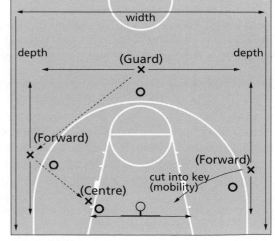

Diagram 5: a 4 v 4 game

An example from football – a 3-5-2 formation

The use of a 3-5-2 formation in football is an example of how a strategy can be adapted to try to bring about individual and team improvement. The extra midfielder in the 3-5-2 formation is designed to give the team extra width. As a result of the extra width, this formation should lead to opportunities to create depth in attack. It should also mean that the pattern of play is more adaptable. A midfield player now has more mobility to make a stronger forward run, leaving less of a gap behind than would be the case with a 4-4-2. (Study diagram 6.)

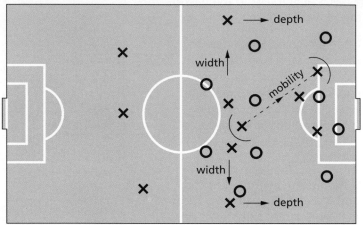

Diagram 6: Width, Depth and Mobility

One crucial question is raised by using the 3-5-2 formation: who should play in the wide midfield positions?

Should they be players who have been full backs in other formations? They are better at defending when necessary and so will help their defence. This would be evident when they close down opposing players and restrict their space.

Should they instead be players who have previously played in more attacking roles? They are better at going forward into attacking positions. This would be evident when they take on defenders and provide good quality crosses.

Another question concerns the three defenders:

Should they be players familiar with playing in the centre of defence, who now take on additional wide defensive responsibilities? They are strong players who are good at tackling and heading. However, they may not be very quick – this means that when they are taken out into wider, more open areas of the pitch, faster attackers can expose their speed limitations.

These considerations should be applied to all positions in the team. Within this 3-5-2 formation, team changes may be made based on your team's tactics and on the perceived quality of the opposition. Changes may also be made to the role you play within the team, even though the overall formation remains the same.

One feature of any formation is that players require to **co-operate**, **support** and **effectively** communicate with each other. Consider the two diagrams on the next page. These diagrams illustrate how in football defenders require to support and communicate with each other to prevent the attacking team playing a ball in behind the defenders. In diagram 7 the two defenders are too far apart and level with each other (square). In this position the player with the ball can play a pass which would allow a quick attacker to gain possession of the ball and proceed towards the opposition goal. However, as diagram 8 highlights, if the two defenders supported and effectively communicated with one another then they could have been closer together, have provided cover for each other and aligned themselves to provide better depth in defence. In this formation the attacker would be less likely to be able to proceed towards the opposition goal.

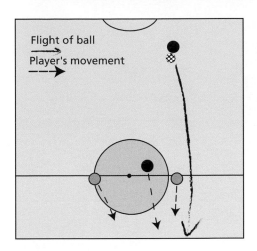

Diagram 7

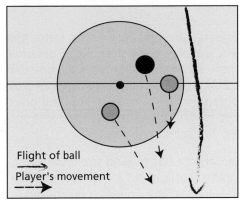

Diagram 8

An example from dance

Other considerations are important in other activities. In dance, effective communication is often important in the constructive development and presentation of a performance. You need to be willing to work with others from the group's first ideas through improvisation, to agreed final form.

When working together in designing a dance performance, it is beneficial if those in the group are receptive to new ideas and can work well in conjunction with others. Being able to work successfully in this way will help lead to a positive ethos developing within the group.

Effective communication is also important when it comes to presenting your performance. Each dancer has a part to play in demonstrating different expressions and feelings within different motifs.

 Consider examples during your own activities of when you and your colleagues have adapted existing strategies to try to improve both your individual and your team's effectiveness.

 Explain the formations you have used and adapted in one activity on your course.

Tactical and design elements

Tactical elements

A tactic is a specific way of carrying out a particular strategy you are using. When you apply different tactics will often depend upon the time within a game and the score within a game. The overall aim of a tactic is to play to your individual and team's/group's strengths, and attempt to exploit your opponents' weaknesses. Tactics can be adapted within a strategy when necessary.

In basketball there are two main defensive strategies: man-to-man and zone defence. Once you have considered which type of defence you are using, you then make specific tactical decisions.

Man-to-man defence

In a man-to-man defence your responsibility is to mark a particular player. Once your opposing player moves into an attacking position, you mark her and attempt to stay between her and the basket. When you do this, tactically, will often depend upon her position and on the state of the game. For example, if your team is trailing with only a minute left, you would wish to chase the game and begin to apply marking pressure on your opponent. You would pick her up when she crosses the halfway line rather than when she moves into the final attacking third.

Zone defence

A zone defence is based on marking an area, rather than a player. The position you play is the main factor determining the area you mark. There are three major types of zone defence: 1-3-1, 1-2-2 and 2-3. (You may have experience of playing in these different formations. If so, you can link your practical experience of these formations in an individual and/or team capacity to your understanding of them.)

Each type of zone defence has its own strengths and weaknesses. Diagrams 9, 10, and 11 show the position players would typically adopt when the opposing guards are bringing the ball up the court.

In these diagrams the defence's areas of weakness are shaded. Notice how these differ for each type of zone defence. Your initial choice of a defensive formation may be based on experience from previous games. However, in order to counteract the strengths of the opposition, it may be necessary to adapt your defensive tactics and change your formation during the game.

A 1-3-1 zone defence (see diagram 9) is a very strong defence to adopt if the attacking team has a good high-post player working along the free-throw line setting up and initiating attacks. Having three defenders close to this area helps to counteract this strength in the opposition. The 1-3-1 is weak against attacking players cutting at speed to the basket and approaching defensive players X_2 and X_4 from behind.

The 1-2-2 zone defence (see diagram 10) is very good at protecting court coverage around the perimeter. It is a strong defence to use against a team with successful longer distance shooters, especially when they shoot from wide positions. However, it is weak once the opposition has worked the ball past the defensive free-throw line (as it is relatively easy to set up cuts into the basket).

A 2-3 zone defence (see diagram 11) is strong both against an effective high-post player and against cuts from the side. It is weak against good shooters, especially when shots are taken from positions just to the sides of the defending guards.

Even though a zone defence marks an area, the team as a unit still needs to move and adjust its position as the opposition moves the ball around the perimeter of the zone.

 These basketball examples of tactical applications provide you with the type of detail about strategy you require. Consider different ways of adjusting existing tactics and comparing different strategies in the activities you are following.

 Explain the tactical elements you have considered and adapted within one activity on your course.

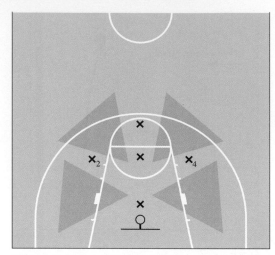

Diagram 9: a 1-3-1 zone defence

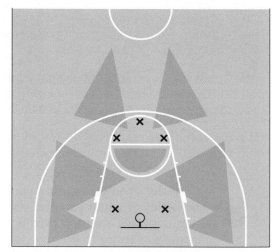

Diagram 10: a 1-2-2 zone defence

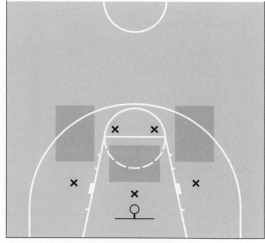

Diagram 11: a 2-3 zone defence

Design elements

Design elements include considerations of the overall **design**, **form** and **style** in a performance. They are particularly important in dance and often in floor work in gymnastics.

Design

The overall design in a performance involves compositional considerations (for example the linking elements in a performance, including the use of space and the dynamics involved within movements).

When using space in a performance you may wish to include different space qualities such as direct (focusing on a specified path) or flexible (with wavy undulating movements). You may also vary some of the dynamics involved in your performance (e.g. movements that differ by being slow, quick or strong). By altering the dynamics involved you can begin to suggest mood within a performance (e.g. quick movements may suggest being happy and full of energy).

By altering the dynamics involved and other overall design elements (such as use of the body and spatial relationships to other performers) you can begin to develop different movement motifs and themes within your performance.

Form

Form involves considering how a performance is organised. In dance, different forms include binary, ternary, rondo and canon. You would use different forms to best enhance your performance. For example, if your dance performance is choreographed to music you may find that it benefits your dance performance to come together during the music chorus.

The rondo form has an **(A)B(A)C(A)D(A)** pattern: a common movement A is followed by a different movement B. Movement A is then repeated before a different movement C occurs. Movement A is returned to before movement D occurs. The rondo form is often used when you have different movements joined together by a common movement pattern. It is similar to a song that has separate verses and a common chorus. This form can be useful when there are many changing relationships within a dance performance. It can help both performers and the audience to understand and appreciate fully the whole performance.

Style

The style used within a certain dance could include different variables. It could refer to the different styles available overall, including modern, Scottish or ethnic. It could also refer to different styles within a certain type of dance, for example within Scottish Country dance there are many different styles, including reel and jig.

Different ideas and themes in dance can be expressed by a motif. Motifs include:

- straightforward movements, e.g. parts of the body being used for travelling, turning and weight transfer and also for leading movements and points of contact with others.
- different speeds (fast, medium, slow) and tempo
- use of space in terms of level (high, medium, low) and direction (forward, diagonal, curved)
- your spatial relationship to others involved in the dance performance (side-by-side, close together, opposite).

Motifs link together to make a phrase. Phrases link together to form a sequence.

 Explain the design elements you have considered and adapted within one activity on your course.

AREA 4 STRUCTURES, STRATEGIES AND COMPOSITION

6

Choreography and composition

Common considerations within choreography and composition are the importance of **timing**, **precision** and **improvisation** in performance. These considerations enable your performance to be interpreted easily, and to show different emotions and moods to be projected in your presentation. They also allow a range of movements to be improvised and developed.

Consider picture A below of four dancers. They are temporally still and holding a balance. The balance is improvised (made up) and unusual. If you focus on the top two dancers, the emotion and image the dancers are trying to project is one of control and strength.

Contrast this picture with picture B of the two dancers. What emotion and mood do you consider that they are trying to project? Discuss your answer with classmates and your teacher. You will probably consider that whilst the picture of the four dancers projects control and strength the picture of the two dancer's instead expresses sensitivity.

Area	Structures, Strategies and Composition
Key Concept 3	Information processing, problem-solving and decision-making when working to develop and improve performance

In this Key Concept you **examine in detail** the importance of evaluating the effectiveness of current structures, strategies or movement compositions in individual, team or group situations. The evaluation process is enhanced by considering how to adapt and refine structures, strategies and movement compositions in response to performance demands.

Here are three examples on pages 89 to 91 of how evaluating the effectiveness of different structures, strategies or movement compositions has taken place in different individual, team and group activities both **before** and **during** performance.

Example 1: An Individual Activity – Spin Bowling in Cricket

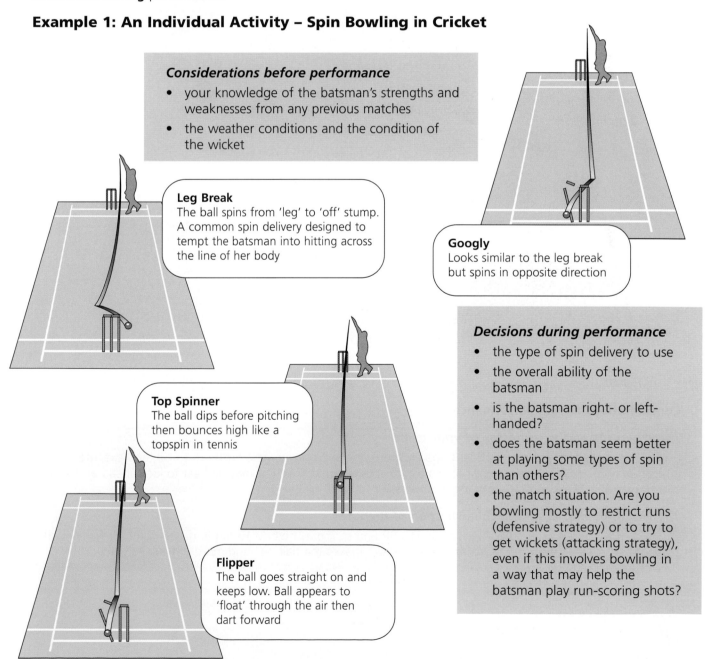

Considerations before performance
- your knowledge of the batsman's strengths and weaknesses from any previous matches
- the weather conditions and the condition of the wicket

Leg Break
The ball spins from 'leg' to 'off' stump. A common spin delivery designed to tempt the batsman into hitting across the line of her body

Googly
Looks similar to the leg break but spins in opposite direction

Top Spinner
The ball dips before pitching then bounces high like a topspin in tennis

Flipper
The ball goes straight on and keeps low. Ball appears to 'float' through the air then dart forward

Decisions during performance
- the type of spin delivery to use
- the overall ability of the batsman
- is the batsman right- or left-handed?
- does the batsman seem better at playing some types of spin than others?
- the match situation. Are you bowling mostly to restrict runs (defensive strategy) or to try to get wickets (attacking strategy), even if this involves bowling in a way that may help the batsman play run-scoring shots?

Example 2: A team activity – attacking in rugby union

In this example the forwards have won possession for the backs from a set play. The ball has been quickly passed from the scrum half (no. 9) to the stand off (no. 10) and on to you, the inside centre (no. 12). In a matter of seconds, you have to make certain key decisions. The overall aim of all strategies at this point is to take possession of the ball further forward with the final aim on most occasions being to score a try.

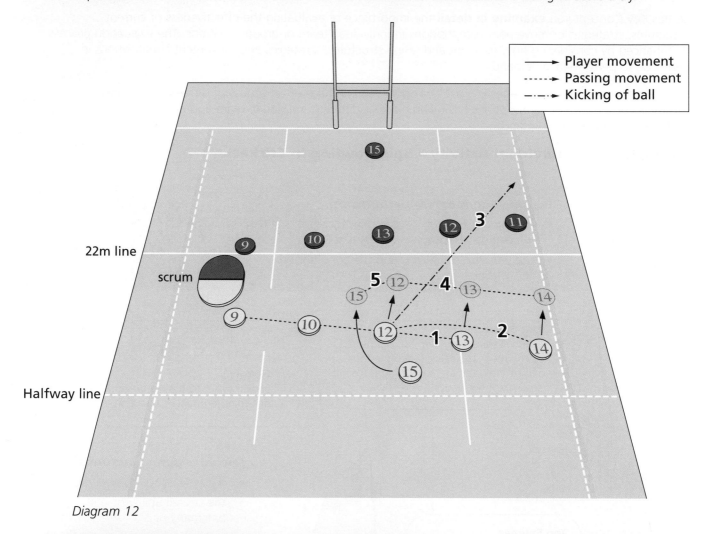

Diagram 12

Considerations before performance

The strengths and weaknesses of your team

If your backs are fast, strong, confident and elusive runners, it may be best for them to run and execute intricate passing manoeuvres. If your forwards are your major strength, it may be best to kick ahead and let your forwards run on and tackle to regain possession.

The weather conditions and the condition of the pitch

In very windy conditions accurate kicking is difficult and so it may be best to run and pass the ball. A very wet pitch makes running with the ball very difficult. It also makes the ball wet and more difficult to catch.

Decisions during performance

Your action with the ball

e.g. pass the ball along the line to the outside centre (no. 13), option 1, or even directly to the winger (no. 14), option 2, or kick the ball, option 3. Combinations of moves are possible: for example, to try to run and break the tackle of the first defender and then pass the ball, option 4; a switch move involving the full back (no. 15) to change the angle of attack is also possible, option 5.

Your position

You can see from diagram 12 that play is in the attacking half in this example. You are, generally, more likely to run and pass the ball from an attacking position than to kick the ball. If possession were in your defensive half then a long defensive kick might be the best option.

The width and length of the pitch

If you are close to the side touchline then a switch move to the full back would be an effective way of trying to keep the ball in play.

The time and score in the game

If there were only a few minutes to go and you were needing to score quickly to gain the lead then the most attacking option would be selected, even though it may be the most risky. For example, trying to miss out the outside centre (no. 13) and pass directly to the winger (no. 14). If you were in your defensive half and you had a large lead, you may be quite content to kick the ball into your opponents' half. They would then need to reorganise their attack and begin again, taking up time in the process.

Example 3: A group activity – use of composition in dance

Considerations before performance

the performance space. You may be performing in a new space. Checking the floor layout and/or stage lighting may be important considerations.

Decisions during performance

These will be relatively few if you are following a planned performance. However, it may be necessary to make some slight adjustments during performance (e.g. to your alignment with other dancers during different parts of the performance). You may also need to make some slight adjustments to your timing (e.g. speeding up or slowing down slightly to ensure that you are in time with other dancers).

Timing and Decision-making

From these examples you can see that in some activities more time is available for decision-making than in others. What kinds of decisions you make often depend on whether the skills involved in the activity are open or closed.

Making Effective Decisions Under Pressure

A further factor which is important in evaluating performance is to consider how to react and respond when under pressure. Consider this example from association football. Diagram 13 highlights how the team reacted when the opposing team had a free kick just outside the penalty area. In this example, a goal is scored.

When a further free kick is awarded the team reacts (diagram 14) by placing a defender on the goal line. Consequently, this allows the goalkeeper to position himself in the same starting position. However, when the free kick is taken he can concentrate on moving to one side only (if necessary) as he realises the other side of the goal is covered by his own defender. This would be an example of making an effective decision when under pressure. It shows evidence of problem-solving. This often involves making perceptive and creative (new) decisions which you had previously not considered.

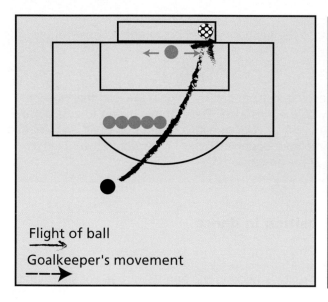

Flight of ball
———▶
Goalkeeper's movement
– – –▶

Diagram 13

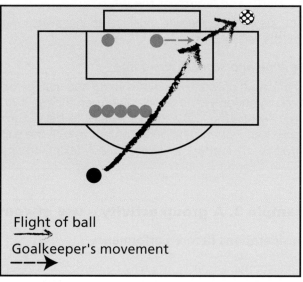

Flight of ball
———▶
Goalkeeper's movement
– – –▶

Diagram 14

  Explain how effective your individual/team/group decision-making has been one activity from your course. Explain the effects upon your performance when you were required to perform under pressure.

Course assessment: revision questions

These revision questions are designed to help you improve your content knowledge (the wheel's hub – see pages 11 to 13) and to help you check how well you are progressing. Model answers are provided at the back of this book. Most questions can be answered within a few lines but some are a little more demanding.

Tip: Ensure your answers are about **your performance** in an activity from **your course.**

Structures, Strategies and Composition

1. Explain the links between structure and strategy and between structure and composition.

2. Give one example of changing the tempo of play within an activity in a chosen structure/strategy.

3. Give one example of using space effectively within a structure/composition.

4. For one team activity, explain how the physical attributes of your players influenced the different roles and responsibilities of your team.

5. Explain the importance of width, depth and mobility within a team game.

6. Explain the importance of width, depth and mobility within an individual activity.

7. Explain the importance of effective communication within a team game.

8. Explain some of the ways in which you could use choreographic ideas to enhance your performance.

9. Choose one activity. Explain two decisions you made in planning for your performance and two decisions you made during performance.

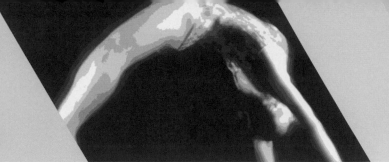

7 UNIT AND COURSE ASSESSMENT IN ANALYSIS AND DEVELOPMENT OF PERFORMANCE

Preparing for your Unit and Course Assessment

Developing Individual Answers

You may find that answering questions in Physical Education is different from answering questions in other subjects. This is because there is no single correct answer to any PE question. For example, in Higher Level Mathematics, you try to work out definite correct answers. However, your answers in Physical Education will be unique to you. This can make answering PE questions appear difficult to begin with. However, with practice and a clear understanding of what is being asked for, you can achieve success.

This section will help you by providing:

detailed advice about how to develop your answers for both Unit and Course Assessments

example answers in each of the four areas of Analysis and Development of Performance areas at Intermediate 2 and Higher Level

Course examples

Different centres (schools and colleges) will link activities to areas of Analysis and development of Performance in a number of ways. This ensures that the answers you develop will be unique to you. In the first example below, Centre A has organised the course as follows:

Centre A

Hockey	– *Preparation of the Body*
Gymnastics	– *Skills and Techniques*
Basketball	– *Structures, Strategies and Composition*

In this next example, you can see that Centre B has different activities and areas of Analysis and Development of Performance combinations:

Centre B

Volleyball	– *Performance Appreciation*
Athletics	– *Preparation of the Body*
Badminton	– *Skills and Techniques*
Hockey	– *Structures, Strategies and Composition*

There are clear design differences between these examples. Centres have different combinations in order to take into account the interests of students and the range of facilities available. In the first example, Centre A has combined three activities with the minimum (three out of four) areas of Analysis and Development of Performance. In the second example, Centre B has covered four activities and has linked each of these to a different area of Analysis and Development of Performance.

There are further similarities and differences in these outlines. Both centres have Hockey in their Courses. However, Centre A has linked hockey to *Preparation of the Body*, whilst Centre B has linked hockey to *Structures, Strategies and Composition*. Both centres have *Skills and Techniques*. However, Centre A's students will answer *Skills and Techniques* questions by considering their gymnastics experience, whilst Centre B's students will answer *Skills and Techniques* questions by considering their badminton experience.

Check that you are sure of how activities link to different areas of Analysis and Development of Performance in your course.

How you are assessed

You will be assessed both during the year (Unit assessment) and at the end of the year (Course assessment). You will be required to complete the following Outcomes and Performance Criteria (PCs)

Performance

For Performance, there is one Outcome. It is to:

'demonstrate effective performance in challenging contexts'.

The Performance Criteria are:

a. A broad performance repertoire is apparent

b. Appropriate decisions are made in challenging performance contexts

c. Control and fluency are demonstrated in performance

Whichever activities you participate in during Higher Still Physical Education your performance should aim to develop your repertoire (range) of skills and techniques, decision-making and control and fluency. Consider these two examples from swimming and volleyball. These examples describe the type of Performance abilities you require.

Swimming example

Repertoire	Decision-making	Control and Fluency
You should be competent in most of the key elements of the two major strokes (frontcrawl, backcrawl or breaststroke). This should be shown in your body position, leg action, arm action, breathing and timing when swimming. Starts should be appropriate to stroke and with an effective flight, entry and glide phase. There should be little loss of momentum as the body completes turns in any of the three major strokes. You should be able to maintain you pace to the finish.	The performance of each stroke should be in demanding contexts where the key elements of each stroke are sustained during the swim. This should be reflected in the interval times taken. Swimming should be against performers of similar ability over distances from 50 m to 200 m. This could involve intra- or inter-class, inter-house or inter-school galas or special events such as qualifying heats for club events.	You should show a high degree of control and fluency in each key aspect of the major strokes. In frontcrawl and backcrawl, for example, the body position should be streamlined with the leg action alternating and continuous, balancing the movements of the arms. Breathing should not affect the fluency of the stroke pattern and should be regular and controlled. The timing should be smooth, balanced and constant.

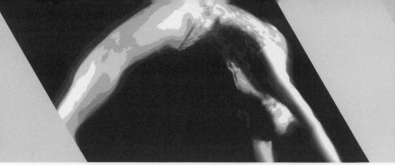

Volleyball example

Repertoire	Decision-making	Control and Fluency
The repertoire (range) evident should include: • Serving • Reception and Passing • Setting • Attacking spike • Net and floor defence Performance at this level is highlighted by effective dynamic balance when moving and making any necessary adjustments to body positions when playing a variety of different shots in games such as 4 v 4 and 6 v 6. Can show effective use of weight transfer to generate both power and control in different skills and techniques.	You can make effective performance decisions during demanding and often competitive games, which involve a variety of options. For example, selecting and combining skills to gain a tactical/strategic advantage. A keen sense of anticipation is evident. Some variation is possible both as planned and at other times through reacting to circumstances, e.g. blocked spikes, etc.	Most actions and patterns are smooth flowing and are controlled, economic and efficient. Most skills show a high level of control and fluency in play, e.g. most skills are automatic. Effective preparation, action and recovery in skills are evident. Some special qualities are apparent, e.g. effective use of deception, disguise, creative application of skill and natural flair when possible. Can usually retain good control when under pressure.

Your performance is assessed in two activities. Each activity is marked out of 20 marks. You require to gain 11 marks or more to achieve the Performance Unit. The two marks out of 20 you achieve are added together to arrive at your final Performance mark for the Course award. For example, if you score 17 marks for one activity and 14 for the second activity the final Performance mark you achieve would be 31 marks out of the 40 marks available.

Your performance work is **assessed on a continuous basis** throughout the session by your teacher(s). As your performance is judged continuously, work out an **improvement plan** for your level of performance.

Ensure that you know the two activities in your course that count towards your final Assessment. For example, if gymnastics, swimming and basketball are the three activities in your course, work out which two are most likely to be included in your final grade. Concentrate on these two outside your centre for performance improvement. If your ability is roughly equal across both activities, ensure you spend time developing each of them. Check your judgements with your teacher.

Check on your performance profile. If you are a very high level performer in one activity, the development of your second activity may increase your mark on the performance scale when it comes to aggregating your marks.

Make sure your performance practice is meaningful. Try to evaluate your performance on an ongoing basis using valid methods for analysing performance.

Plan ahead (e.g. by booking facilities and by informing other participants). Time is precious! If you are playing against an opponent of a similar ability in badminton, ensure your on-court time is adequate for the ongoing development of particular aspects of your performance. Check that your partner (or opponent) knows her/his role in different performance settings.

Analysis and Development of Performance

Unit Assessment

The assessment instrument for this Unit is an assignment. The assignment provides a record of your work as you investigate and develop an aspect of your performance. The assignment process is structured to allow you to record each stage of your analysis, and to show how relevant Key Concept knowledge was understood and applied in the planning of a programme of work. Finally, an evaluation of the effectiveness of the analysis and development process is completed.

The assignment requires you to apply knowledge from a minimum of two Key Concepts from a specific area of Analysis and Development of Performance. You should understand how the demands of the Unit assignment link to the process of analysing performance and to specific Key Concepts. The greater detail you use to provide explanations about how you collected information and Key Concepts the better. This will help you to make detailed judgements when analysing performance, to explain how you monitored your performance when training and how you evaluated your chosen course of action.

To complete the assignment, you choose an aspect of your performance from the activities you are taking part in during Physical Education. The programme of work you complete should last for enough time for you to discuss and evaluate how your performance has progressed. You are required to complete **one assignment** from one area of Analysis and Development of Performance.

Timing and duration of assessment

Your teacher will advise you on whether you will complete one assessment of up to one and a half hours or two shorter assessments of up to 45 minutes each. For example, your might complete the first two learning outcomes in your assignment in the first 45 minute assessment and the second two learning outcomes in the second assessment. Your teacher will ensure that you have completed sufficient work before you begin your assessment and provide you with regular feedback about the standard of your assignment answer.

Completing the assignment

To achieve a Unit you must pass each of the four Outcomes in **one** area of Analysis and Development of Performance: *Performance Appreciation*, *Preparation of the Body*, *Skills and Techniques* or *Structures*, *Strategies and Composition*. To achieve each Outcome you need to answer a number of questions which relate to your analysis. Pages 108 and 132 provide example answers at both Intermediate 2 and Higher Level. Try to produce the very best assignment you can. This will help your centre estimate how well you are likely to do in your Course assessment. It will also provide your centre with information that could be used to support an **appeal**. If you are unsuccessful in achieving a Course award when your centre expects you to do so, your centre can appeal on **evidence** collected during the year. This includes your Unit answers and other related coursework. For these reasons, try to ensure that your Unit answers are as full and detailed as possible. If necessary, you are normally allowed one opportunity to be reassessed.

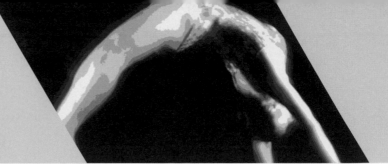

7 UNIT AND COURSE ASSESSMENT IN ANALYSIS AND DEVELOPMENT OF PERFORMANCE

The Unit and Course Assessment process

When completing the assignment, you complete work in a number of different stages. These are:

- *Investigate*: where you explain how a specific aspect of performance was investigated through gathering information

- *Analyse*: where you explain in detail how knowledge from Key Concepts helped you to analyse performance

- *Develop*: where you complete a programme of work and explain how the programme was monitored

- **Review/Evaluate**: where you reflect on the effectiveness of the programme of work and discuss future performance needs.

The assignment stages match the different Outcomes and performance criteria for the Unit. The table below explains the links at both Intermediate 2 and Higher Level.

Intermediate 2

Stage	Outcomes	Performance Criteria
Investigate	1. Explain performance in an activity	(a) Methods selected and used for observing and recording data are valid (b) Data gathered are valid (c) Performance strengths and weaknesses are explained (d) Development needs are explained
Analyse	2. Use Knowledge and Understanding to analyse performance	(a) Relevant Key Concepts and key features are selected and used to analyse performance (b) Relevant information sources are used to plan performance development (c) A programme of work is designed to meet identified needs
Develop	3. Monitor a programme of work	(a) A relevant programme of work to meet identified needs is completed (b) The content of the programme of work is monitored (c) Performance development is monitored
Review	4. Review the analysis and development process	(a) The effectiveness of the analysis and development process is explained (b) The effects on performance are explained (c) Future development needs are explained

Higher Level

Stage	Outcomes	Performance Criteria
Investigate	1. Analyse performance in an activity	(a) Methods selected and used for observing and recording data are valid (b) Data gathered are valid (c) Performance strengths and weaknesses are valid (d) Development needs are analysed
Analyse	2. Use Knowledge and Understanding to analyse performance	(a) Relevant Key Concepts and key features are selected and used to analyse performance in detail (b) Relevant information sources are used effectively to plan performance development (c) A programme of work is designed to effectively address identified needs
Develop	3. Monitor a programme of work	(a) A relevant programme of work to address identified needs is completed (b) The content and demand of the programme of work is monitored (c) Performance development is monitored effectively
Evaluate	4. Evaluate the analysis and development process	(a) The effectiveness of the analysis and development process is discussed (b) The effects on performance are discussed (c) Future development needs are discussed

Tip: At Higher Level, you are required to move from explaining to discussing and from reviewing to evaluating. To help you, try to focus on the effectiveness of your performance improvement and on the processes you completed for analysing your performance.

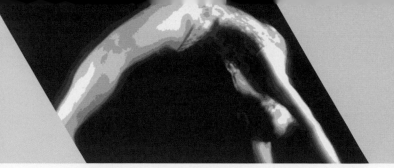

7 UNIT AND COURSE ASSESSMENT IN ANALYSIS AND DEVELOPMENT OF PERFORMANCE

Investigating Performance (Intermediate 2 Level)

At Intermediate 2 Level, your aim is to provide a clear and precise explanation of how you collected information (data) and why the methods used were accurate (valid). This makes it possible for you to **explain** your performance strengths and weaknesses and development needs.

The following stages are important:

• What you did?   • How you did it?   • Where you did it?   • Why you did it?

Study the example below:

Example: Volleyball with Skills and Techniques

Stage	Activity	Record and Description	Notes
What you did?		I collected information on the most important skills in volleyball. These were volleying, digging, serving, spiking and blocking. I recorded my performance during a 4v4 inter-school tournament. For my first look at my performance (initial data), I recorded whether I carried out these skills effectively, with limited effectiveness or ineffectively. I then went on to take a more detailed (specific data) look at the skill of spiking. I did this because my initial data showed that spiking was my least effective skill.	Effectively links between methods of collecting information, how observation and recording will take place and the skills involved have been clearly established.
How you did it?		One of my classmates observed my performance during the inter-school tournament and collected data on my performance during the small-sided games. It was possible for them to record my performance accurately as they had to pay attention to my performance only and not to those of others in the class. This made recording possible. When observing, my classmate stood close to the half of the court I was on so that he/she could closely observe my performance. My classmate had experience of volleyball as he/she is in class: this helped make sure that his/her observations were accurate	Clear reference to the importance of analysing performance in meaningful contexts, i.e. small-sided games, has been mentioned.
Where you did it?		The observation schedules were completed at the local sports centre where the Inter school tournament was taking place. This was a very good venue as the court was a good size for 4 v 4 games of Volleyball. In addition there was a lot of space beside to record results.	Clear reference to where information was collected.
Why you did it?		Collecting data using observation schedules from small-sided games is a way of gaining accurate information about my strengths and weaknesses in different volleyball skills: these are all important for improving performance.	Relevant points about linking observation schedule to own strengths and weaknesses are made.

In the above volleyball example, the **initial data** might look like the table below.

Skill	Effective (✓)	Limited effectiveness (?)	Ineffective (X)
Volley	✓✓✓✓	???	XX
Dig	✓✓✓	??	XX
Serve	✓✓✓✓✓	??	X
Spiking	✓	??	XXXX
Blocking	✓✓✓✓	?	XX

The **focused data** for spiking might look like the observation schedule shown on page 16.

Investigating Performance (Higher Level)

At Higher Level, your aim is to analyse how you collected information (data) and why the methods used for collecting information were valid. This then makes it possible for you to **analyse** your performance strengths and weaknesses and development needs.

There are many different methods of collecting information. Choose methods that will allow you to 'paint a picture' of what you did when performing. You can then provide a detailed analysis of why your methods were appropriate and valid. You will find it useful to consider:

– **the nature and demands of the activity**
– **your specific role and responsibilities within the activity**
– **your current level of performance**
– **the area of Analysis and Development of Performance being studied.**

The purpose of collected information is to provide you with a record of your performance to which you can make further, regular references. Within your explanations, it is often important to have a balance between quantitative (objective, clearly measurable information) and qualitative (subjective, opinion-based information). Achieving this balance helps you to develop depth in your answers. Consider the following example from football where information has been collected about passing ability in a small-sided football game.

Example: Collecting information in football

(Visual picture)	(Verbal written description)	
Football game	**Objective**	**Subjective**
	Most effective/least effective parts of your game as shown by: • number of passes completed • distance and direction of passes • degree of opposition when making passes	Your own thoughts and feelings about how well you played, e.g. • self control during game • level of confidence, anxiety, determination, motivation

In this example, the combination of objective and subjective information about methods of collecting information could add to your explanation's depth. For example, you could explain how making effective and ineffective passes affected your level of confidence throughout the game.

If your data is purely objective or subjective, it might well be less detailed. For example, through concentrating on just the facts and figures of passes you made or through only considering your thoughts and feelings (without considering the frame of reference provided by detailed passing information), parts of the whole 'picture' of your passing would be missing.

> **Tip:** Remember to limit yourself to what the Unit Outcome is asking at this stage of your answer.
> Refer to 'Methods of Collecting Information' on pages 14-20 for further detail on such methods.

Analyse Performance (Intermediate 2 and Higher Level)

For most students, developing a detailed answer based on relevant links to the Key Concepts is the most difficult part of producing a very good answer. From the data you have collected, explained and analysed, you should have a detailed picture and explanation about 'what you did'. Next, you need to explain 'why it was important'. To do this, you need to link your answer through the 'spokes on the wheel' (see pages 11 and 13) to underpin Key Concept content knowledge (the wheel's hub).

A useful way of developing depth in answering is to think firstly of '*painting a picture*' (visualisation) of what you did. This enables you to report next on 'why it was important' (verbalisation). Here is an example:

Example: Volleyball with Skills and Techniques

Visualisation:

Recall

...what you did **...how you did it** **...where you did it** **...why you did it**

Verbalise:

Report 'Why was it important?'

> It was important that I collected information from my whole performance because this gave me a genuine overall view of my strengths and weaknesses. I needed to know how effective my performance was in a game, as opposed to in practice, because this is a better indicator of my true ability. This was my first priority. The collected information showed that my spiking required a more detailed analysis.
>
> Next, I needed to look at methods of collecting information that were both reliable and valid (accurate) for assessing my performance in a volleyball game. I decided that observation schedules would be a useful method, because they would enable analysis of my performance in small-sided volleyball games. I collected some initial information that established whether my skills were effective, of limited effectiveness or ineffective. After this, I made a detailed, specific analysis of my spiking. This analysis broke the skill down into Preparation/Action/Recovery. This allowed a more detailed assessment of my weaknesses.
>
> This method of collecting information (observation schedules) was a suitable method because it was possible for a classmate who had a good level of experience and expertise in volleyball to accurately record my performance.

Clear reference to the importance of analysing performance in meaningful contexts.

Effective links between methods of collecting information, how observation and recording will take place and the skills involved have been established.

Note: The answer is written in the 'first person' ('I did...'). This is important because **your** experience is the basis of your answer.

In your writing, try to move beyond stating established facts to discussing why these facts were important. For example, when writing about principles of training, try to move beyond writing about what specificity and progressive overload are to discussing how you applied **your understanding** of principles of training in the development of your performance. This will help to develop the content of your answers whilst still being based on your performance experience.

When completing your Unit Assessment in the Analysis and Development of Performance Unit you are required to link your answer to **two** Key Concepts. Understanding which two Key Concepts you are focusing on is important. So, check that you are familiar with the Key Concepts in the different areas of Analysis and Development of Performance. The table on page 6 contains all the Key Concepts in each area of Analysis and Development of Performance.

Develop Performance

In developing your performance you should try to regularly monitor and review your performance. The more continuously you check on your progress the better prepared you will be to make any necessary **adaptations** to your training programme. Link your planned performance improvements to your **short- and long-term goals**. Use feedback you gain from monitoring your performance to revise as necessary your goals.

When monitoring your performance you should try to refer to the data you have collected about your performance as often as possible. This will help provide you with accurate information to make comparisons with your more recent performances. Try to ensure that your suggested improvements build upon the data you have collected and your understanding of relevant Key Concepts. Be reasonable and realistic in suggesting improvements.

Review/Evaluate Performance

Ensure that your review of performance includes both **specific and general** aspects of performance. For example, if you are trying to improve serving in table tennis then review both the effectiveness of your serving in table tennis and the effect it has on your overall table tennis game.

In discussing your performance improvements try to link them to the performance abilities which are required within the Performance Unit. Try to relate performance improvement to the repertoire of skills and techniques required, effective decision-making and control and fluency. If you can make these performance connections it will help add to the depth and quality of performance review.

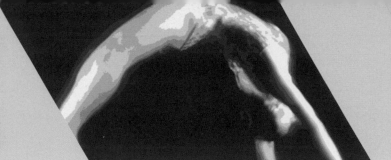

7 UNIT AND COURSE ASSESSMENT IN ANALYSIS AND DEVELOPMENT OF PERFORMANCE

Course Assessment: Examples and Wording of Questions

Course Assessment

Your external Course Assessment at Intermediate 2 takes the form of a two-hour written exam at the end of your Course. Your external Course Assessment at Higher Level takes the form of a two and a half-hour written exam at the end of your Course.

Each of the three answers you complete is out of 20 marks. Hence, your total Course Assessment is out of 60 marks. This total is added to your Performance mark which is out of 40 marks (2 activities, each marked out of 20 marks) to give a final figure out of 100 marks for the entire Course Assessment.

At both levels you are required to answer three questions, each from a different area of Analysis and Development of Performance. Make sure you understand the format of the examination. Any prelim examination you complete should help in this respect.

In your answers you must show the ability to:

- Give clear, full and detailed explanations about your performance

- Show that you understand all relevant Key Concepts and can make sound judgements

- Monitor a programme of work

- Evaluate and analyse performance improvements.

Ensure that your answer is based on the relevant Key Concepts. For example, if you are answering a *Performance Appreciation* question, make sure your answer relates to the Key Concepts in this area that the question is asking about.

Your answers will be marked by Physical Education teachers working for the Scottish Qualifications Authority (SQA). These markers will read your answers thoroughly and award marks based on the ability (competence) that you have shown. The main requirement is that your answers are as **full and detailed** as possible.

The demands of the Unit Assessment are very similar to those of the Course Assessment. Therefore, the better you do at the Unit Assessment, the greater the chance there is of you **transferring** your understanding from your Unit answers to your Course answers.

To produce examination answers that reflect your ability, it is useful to practise answering questions under examination conditions. This will help you to cope with the **time demands** of writing under examination conditions and will test your ability to **retain and recall** the fine detail of your course experiences and the understanding you developed from practical learning.

After you have completed the two Units that make up a Course award there should be time available for you to further practise developing your answers. Use this time productively, in the time before the Course examination.

Examples of Course Questions

Here are four example questions, one from each area of Analysis and Development of Performance. You should be able to see some **differences** and some **similarities** in the way the questions are set out.

1. Performance Appreciation (Higher)

From one activity in your course:

(a) Describe the **nature** and **demands** of the activity, as you worked towards improving the overall **quality** of your performance. — **6**

(b) Explain the major **strengths** and **weaknesses** in the overall **quality** of your performance. — **4**

(c) For the weaknesses identified in part (b) above explain the plan of action you followed to improve your quality of your performance. — **6**

(d) Evaluate the effectiveness of the plan of action you followed in terms of improving the quality of performance. — **4**

(20)

See pages 109 to 111 for a completed answer to this question.

2. Preparation of the Body (Intermediate 2)

Choose **one** activity from your course.

Physical aspects of fitness	Skill-related aspects of fitness	Mental aspects of fitness
cardiorespiratory endurance	reaction time	level of arousal
local muscular endurance	agility	nature of motivation
strength	co-ordination	mental rehearsal
speed	balance	managing stress
power	timing	
flexibility		

(a) Choose **two physical aspects of fitness** and explain their importance in developing your performance in the activity you have chosen. — **6**

(b) Choose one aspect of either **skill-related OR mental aspect of fitness** and explain its importance in developing your performance in the activity you have chosen. — **3**

(c) For one of the aspects of fitness you have chosen in parts (a) or (b) describe how you collected information on this aspect of fitness. — **4**

(d) Explain briefly how you **planned** a training programme for the aspect of fitness you collected information on in part (c). — **3**

(e) Explain briefly how you **evaluated** a training programme for the aspect of fitness you collected information on in part (d). — **3**

(20)

3. Skills and Techniques (Higher)

Choose **one** activity.

When analysing your performance you will have used one of the following methods.

Mechanical analysis   Movement analysis   Consideration of quality

(a) Choose one of the methods above. Explain in detail how this method was useful for collecting information about your performance.   **6**

(b) Using the information collected in part (a), describe of your Analysis of Performance's results.   **4**

(c) Your performance will have been affected by:

   Motivation   Concentration   Feedback

   Explain the importance of **one** of the factors in the development of your performance.   **6**

(d) Explain how you evaluated your performance with regard to the factor chosen in part (c).   **4**

4. Structures, Strategies and Composition (Intermediate 2)

(a) Choose **one** activity. Describe in detail a structure, strategy or composition you have used.   **4**

(b) Describe how you **collected information** about the structure, strategy or composition you have described in part (a).   **4**

(c) Explain the major **strengths** in the structure, strategy or composition you have described in part (a).   **4**

(d) Explain the major weaknesses in the structure, strategy or composition you have described in part (a).   **4**

(e) Describe how you evaluated the structure, strategy or composition you have described in part (a).   **4**

(20)

See pages 132 to 135 for a completed answer to this question.

You should be able to see some **similarities** in each of these questions. They are all meant to be open and accessible. This means that they can be answered from whatever activities and experiences you have had on your course.

You should also be able to see some slight **differences** in the way the questions are set out. The Intermediate 2 Level questions tend to have more sections with a small number of marks for each section. The Higher Level questions tend to have fewer sections but each section is worth more marks.

Types of Questions

There tend to be two types of Course examination questions. There are those where the **process** is clearly apparent from the question's wording. Questions 1 and 4 above are examples of this type of question. In these questions you should be able to see how the different parts of the question link to the four stages involved in the Cycle of Analysis. In answering these questions, ensure that the process you go through in answering them draws upon relevant Analysis and Development of Performance content (Key Concepts) as often as possible.

There are also questions where the **content** of the question is much more prominent. Questions 2 and 3 above are examples of this type of question. In answering these questions ensure that the content of your answer links to relevant Analysis of Performance processes as often as possible.

Wording of Questions

The wording of questions (as well as the marks available) will provide you with an insight into the level of detail required within your answer. Try to take account of the **active verbs** that are included within questions. The diagram below indicates how an increase in the demands of the active verb used will be reflected in the difficulty of the question and the marks available.

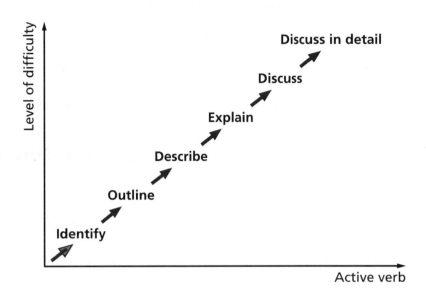

In the Course Examination

Once you have decided which three sections of the exam paper you will answer:

Take time to read all the questions from each section and choose the one you find most straightforward to answer.

Study how the marks are awarded in each question. For example, if the question parts are awarded as 4, 4, 8 and 4 marks, ensure that you are well aware of what is required in the 8-mark section of the question.

Allocate the correct amount of time to each part of each question. Spend more time answering a section worth 8 marks than a section worth 4. Monitor your time closely.

Plan an outline of your answer prior to beginning your answer. Avoid being rushed into starting before your thoughts are complete.

Keep the context of your answer centred on your performance, either as an individual or as part of a group or team.

Ensure your answers avoid repetition. Each question part is asking something specific. You do not have time for unnecessary detail or vague writing.

Try to keep the thread of your answer going. Concentrate only on exactly what the question is asking.

Allocate equal time to each question. You need to complete three good answers. Remember that one poorly answered or half-answered question will lower your overall mark.

Pages 108 to 135 provide four different assessment examples. Close scrutiny of these examples will provide helpful insights into what makes a good answer.

The examples shown include:

- Course Assessment at Higher Level (*Performance Appreciation*)

- Unit Assessment at Intermediate 2 Level (*Preparation of the Body*)

- Unit Assessment at Higher Level (*Skills and Techniques*)

- Course Assessment at Intermediate 2 Level (*Structures, Strategies and Composition*)

For further examples of Course Assessment examples in Higher Still Physical Education at Higher Level you should refer to Leckie and Leckie, Higher Physical Education Specimen Question Papers, 2000, 2001 and 2002.

Course Assessment: Performance Appreciation (Higher)

From **one** activity in your course:

(a) Describe the **nature** and **demands** of the activity, as you worked towards improving the overall **quality** of your performance. **6**

(b) Explain the major **strengths** and **weaknesses** in the overall **quality** of your performance. **4**

(c) For the weaknesses identified in part (b) above explain the plan of action you followed to improve your quality of your performance. **6**

(d) Evaluate the effectiveness of the plan of action you followed in terms of improving the quality of performance. **4**

(20)

Chosen activity: rugby union

(a) Describe the **nature** and **demands** of the activity, as you worked towards improving the overall **quality** of your performance. **6**

Playing rugby has many different demands to consider. Many of the demands are similar for all players in the team but some are specific to individual players who play in particular positions.

The nature of rugby presents its own special challenges. Rugby is directly competitive and this means that players need to have personal and physical qualities in order to succeed. Personal qualities such as determination, courage and the ability to work as part of a team are required by all players. For example, tackling requires courage.

Working as part of a team involves agreeing how the team is going to play to its strengths. Because rugby teams have 15 players, it would be chaotic if each player played for him or herself instead of for the team. As a result, it will be necessary for forwards and backs, the two major groups of players in a team, to agree how the game is going to be played. Playing will often involve the forwards winning possession of the ball, then passing it quickly to the backs. Playing as part of a team will also be important in determining the speed and tempo of the game. For example, it would help us to decide whether we to play a fast, open, attacking game or a close, tight, defensive game. I play as a stand-off half (number 10) so my role is crucial in decisions about following a game plan.

Physical qualities are also needed but these will differ according to a player's position. In my role, I need to be quite quick and quite strong. Other players, mostly the forwards (numbers 1–8), need to be particularly strong. For the backs that line up outside me (numbers 11–15), it is useful if they are quick. The scrum half (number 9) and I are often referred to as the 'link' players in the team as we link the forwards and backs. As well as being quite quick and strong, we also all need to sometimes show a lightness of touch, for example when we or the forwards set the ball back in rucks and when the backs are passing.

Good introduction of the link between nature of activity and personal qualities – more development of this link was required.

The knowledge shown about the importance of working as a team is very good and shows that the student has an awareness of different roles and responsibilities.

Useful team description of physical qualities is set out. More development of some of the physical qualities required with further game examples would have been useful.

4 marks out of 6 awarded: Clear, full and occasionally detailed description of nature and demands of performance.

Tip: For more marks, you should give more detailed descriptions of physical demands and qualities. Further consideration of special qualities such as courage, which is mentioned briefly, would have been useful.

(b) Explain the major **strengths** and **weaknesses** in the overall **quality** of your performance.   **4**

I have been playing rugby for many years. Overall, I consider that my performance has steadily improved. However, I think that some qualities within my performance are showing better progress than others. Physically, I have always been strong in the tackle and I have always taken responsibility for tackling when necessary even though I am a fair bit smaller than many other players.

My teachers and coaches have also been pleased with my commitment to the team and my intentions towards playing to the agreed team plan, whether this is based on either a fast, passing game or tighter, kicking game. As a result, my **personal** commitment to the team has never been in doubt. I have also managed to stay calm under pressure and this has been reflected in the way that I have encouraged my team-mates rather than criticised them during the game.

My most noticeable weaknesses are in the **technical** and **special** qualities involved in my performance. When we are playing a fast, attacking game, the backs tend to line up in a 'flat line' which involves being close to the other team. This is a high-risk strategy. The idea is that by playing this way we can put pressure on the opposing players as early as possible to break over their gain line and maintain an attacking advantage. We prefer this to playing in a deeper line and often kicking the ball forward which would risk giving away possession at an early stage. My technical weakness when playing this way is that I can lack consistency when having to make moves quickly. I tend to rush and this can lead to losing possession through choosing poor options, such as trying to make a break when there is little space available or making a poor pass. I feel that developing some special performance qualities such as flair and deception would create uncertainty in the opposing team.

Useful introduction about the practice plan of action that is intended is outlined

The link between practices and game settings is well made, However, more detail on the progressions involved within the practices and how as a result the practices became increasingly demanding would have been useful.

Some useful points about the relevance of the practices are made.

4 marks out of 4 awarded:
Clear, full and detailed
explanation that uses a full
range of relevant concepts to
make detailed judgements.

(c) For the weaknesses identified in part (b) above explain the plan of action you followed to improve your quality of performance.

6

The plan of action I followed was to undertake some problem-solving practices which revolved around making split-second decisions and adapting to what happens after decisions have been made. Clear objectives were set for these practices: these were set out and agreed by the teachers and the players. For example, we would set up practices where the aim was to get beyond the gain line as soon as possible. Other practices involved passing the ball along the line as quickly as possible. Some practices involved one of 'our' players deliberately running straight at 'opposing' players and trying to knock them over. This is called a 'crash ball'. If 'our' player is tackled, then we try to 'recycle' the ball as quick as possible and keep play moving forward.

The key point about all these practices is that they were meant to be as near to a full game as possible. The degree of difficulty in these practices was altered in various ways. For example, we altered how flat we played. The flatter our line was, the more difficult the practices were. Difficulty was also added by the 'opposing' players playing full opposition in the practices or reduced slightly by playing against a bit less than full opposition. The main idea behind the practices was that they had to have a quality focus. As a result, the time we spent on these practices was relatively short: usually about 15 minutes within an overall 75-minute training session.

These practices were very useful for me as they specifically addressed my technical weaknesses. I had to make decisions under time pressure and select options that I could consistently carry out well. It also gave me the opportunity to work out solutions that were unusual and that I had not tried before. As a result, I became more confident at trying out new moves for real during a game.

> Useful introduction about the practice plan of action that is intended is outlined

> The link between practices and game settings is well made. However, more detail on the progressions involved within the practices and how as a result the practices became increasingly demanding would have been useful.

> Some useful points about the relevance of the practices are made.

> **4 marks out of 6 awarded:** A clear, full and occasionally detailed explanation about a course of action that is likely to lead to improvement is outlined.

(d) Evaluate the effectiveness of the plan of action you followed in terms of improving the quality of performance.

4

The evaluation of the effectiveness of the training programme will only be possible after we have played a range of different types of rugby games which call for the implementation of different types of alignment amongst the back players. As a collective back unit, the training exercises appear to be useful because they have made us focus on taking what we have understood from our practices out onto the pitch.

To make more definite judgements, it will also be useful to consider in future game analyses how well we played after longer phases of action. This would mean that, for example, even if we played a 'crash ball' strategy the initial first phase move might not get us to much progress. However, we might be able to recycle the ball and make effective progress in the second phase of our attack.

> A recognition of the need to reference practices against game performance is mentioned but regrettably not included with supporting game statistics, etc.

> Some relevant areas of game performance for evaluation are indicated.

> **2 marks out of 4 awarded:** Some clear and satisfactory suggestions for improvement are outlined.

Total: 14 out of 20 marks awarded.

Unit Assessment: Preparation of the Body (Intermediate 2)

Your Unit assignment takes you through different analysis stages. The Cycle of Analysis is one popular approach. See diagram 2 on page 11.

You begin your assignment by selecting the activity, area of Analysis of Performance and specific aspect of performance you will be trying to improve.

Activity: Hockey **Area of Analysis of Performance**: Preparation of the Body

Specific aspect of performance analysed: Skill-related fitness (agility) when dribbling in hockey.

You then briefly explain the significance of this aspect to your whole performance.

> The main effect of my poor agility is that I get caught in possession and then the other team has the opportunity to get the ball. When dribbling, I can usually keep the stick close to the ball and as a result the ball is usually under control. This would indicate that my skill was quite good. It is just that the other players chasing me had caught me up. This was due to my poor agility — the ability to move my body quickly and precisely.

You then need to begin the **Investigation** process through collecting information about your performance. There are a number of methods of collecting information which might be useful for you to consider. Many of these are outlined on pages 14 to 20. Refer to these when choosing the best method for your Investigation.

In this example, game analysis sheets have been used for both the initial and focused levels of data collection.

Initial level of data collection

I had the following game analysis sheet completed. This allowed me to find out about my speed in a seven-a-side hockey game lasting 30 minutes each half.

Game Analysis Sheet

Team: Scotstown Academy **Role**: Attacker
Opposition: Central High School **Date**: 25/11/05

✓ = effective

Type of speed measured	Role in game	1st half	2nd half
Getting free in attack (Short sprint)	Attacking	✓✓✓✓✓	✓✓✓
Getting free in attack (Long sprint)	Attacking	✓✓✓	✓✓✓
Dribbling (Short sprint)	Attacking	✓✓✓	✓
Dribbling (Long sprint)	Attacking	✓✓✓✓✓	
Getting back in defence (Short sprint)	Attacking	✓✓✓✓	✓✓✓✓
Getting back in defence (Long sprint)	Attacking	✓✓✓✓	✓✓✓

Personal review

From this data I could find out roughly how fit I was for sprinting in a seven-a-side hockey game. As a forward, I try to get free by losing my marker and by dribbling the ball forward into space. When defending, I also need to get back to help my team in midfield. The results show that I can mostly keep sprinting pretty well throughout the game but my dribbling gets less useful as the game goes on.

Focused level of data collection

I had the following game analysis sheet completed. This allowed me to find out about my sprinting when dribbling in a seven-a-side hockey game lasting 30 minutes each half.

Game Analysis Sheet

Team: Scotstown Academy
Opposition: Central High School

Role: Attacker
Date: 25/11/05

✓ = effective   ✗ = ineffective

Dribbling speed measured	Role in game	1st half	2nd half
Dribbling unopposed (Short sprint)	Attacking in space	✓✓	✓✓✗✗
Dribbling unopposed (Long sprint)	Attacking in space	✓✗	✓✗✗
Dribbling opposed (Short sprint)	Attacking under pressure	✓✗✗	✓✗✗
Dribbling opposed (Long sprint)	Attacking under pressure	✓✓✗	✗✗
Reverse stick dribble	Wide in attack	✓✗	

Personal review

I looked at my dribbling speed in more detail. I looked at how often in a game I was able to sprint and dribble well and how often I was ineffective in doing this.

Once you have collected this data, you can then go on to answer the Unit Outcome questions.

Remember: With your Unit Assessments you are able to directly use the data that you have collected in the answering of your question. The answers to Outcomes 1 – 4 (pages 114 to 120) are based on the data collected on the game analysis sheets above.

UNIT AND COURSE ASSESSMENT EXAMPLES

Outcome 1: Explain Performance in an activity

- PC (a) Methods selected and used for observing and recording data are valid

- PC (b) Data gathered are valid

- PC (c) Performance strengths and weaknesses are explained

- PC (d) Development needs are explained

Outcome questions

Explain the main information you collected from the data.

> **Tip:** This is an ideal opportunity for you to build an answer around What you did?, How you did it?, Where you did it? and Why you did it? (See page 100.)

Student example answer

Teacher example comment

I think the way I collected information worked well. It was important that I collected information about what I was doing in a full game, rather than in my practices. The first game analysis sheet allowed me to look at my sprint speed both when I was just sprinting and also when I was trying to sprint and dribble the ball at the same time. The second sheet allowed me to consider my dribbling in more detail. This was good as dribbling was the part of the game I was poorest at doing.

The importance of using whole performance (games) for collecting information is well made as is the transfer between initial (general) and focused (specific) data.

Explain why the methods you used to record data were valid.

The layout of the sheets was helpful. The sheets were well set out and easy to fill in, even during a fast game. This is because they were clear and well set out with plenty of space within the boxes. They also allowed me to add my own comments on how well I thought I had done. This will be helpful for me to look back on later.

Relevant points about how the observation sheets are to be completed are outlined.

Explain how your data helped you recognise your performance strengths and weaknesses.

The data has shown me a lot of useful things about my level of fitness in hockey. Basically, I found out more and more detailed information as I went on. To start with, from my initial data I found that I had two problems.

The first one was that I seemed to make fewer sprints as the game went on. You can see this from the reduced number of ticks for the second half as compared to the first half. The second problem I found was that I was less effective at dribbling quickly with the ball than I was at straight sprinting. Being able to dribble quickly is important in my position.

The results of my data were quite useful for me. This is good because it told me accurately what I needed to work on. My problems seemed to be that I got tired as the game went on. This could let my performance down. More importantly, it showed that my agility when dribbling in hockey was not very good.

The correct identification of two relevant performance issues has been explained.

Explain how your data helped you recognise your development needs.

> The main thing is that I needed to work on was my agility. I could sprint quite well, better in the first half than second half, but when dribbling the ball and running in a different shape and changing direction a lot, I found it difficult to keep my speed up. I also seemed to be slow at turning: this was shown by my focused level data. My mistake rate was quite high. I needed to work on agility.
>
> I tended to slow up too much to turn quickly. I think that sometimes I was driving off the wrong foot and this affected my balance when moving. For example, when dribbling forward with the ball on my left hand side, I would often try to knock the ball back over to my right hand side on the move. Often I would be doing this when my left foot (instead of my right foot) was forward. This was complicated and awkward. Being able to change direction is important for forwards because it allows them to get free of and go past defenders, either with or without the ball.
>
> The midfield players in my team rely on me, one of the forwards, to make attacking breaks and to keep possession of the ball when I'm tying to get deep into the attacking half of the pitch. To do this, I needed to work on my agility. Better agility meant less risk of getting caught in possession and remaining in control of the ball as I would be able to move quicker and stay in better balance. If I could keep my agility at a good rate through the game this would help as well.

> The usefulness of the initial data in highlighting a specific performance issue has been quite carefully explained.

> Further clarity about the importance of agility to forward play in hockey is outlined.

> Relevant link to skill-related aspect of fitness and its importance within a game of hockey is made. Some further game-related examples of how this affected game performance would have been useful

Outcome 2: Use Knowledge and Understanding to Analyse Performance

PC (a)   Relevant Key Concepts and key features are selected and used to analyse performance

PC (b)   Relevant information sources are used to plan performance development

PC (c)   A programme of work is designed to meet identified needs

To complete this next stage of the assignment you need to link your data to relevant Key Concepts. This will help you to analyse your performance and plan a development programme. Each assignment answer requires to link to two Key Concepts. You might find it useful to specify the key features you are using to help your analyse as well.

Key Concept 1	Application of different types of fitness in the development of activity specific performance
Key feature	Examine the performance requirement and related fitness needs for selected activities
Key Concept 2	Principles and methods of training
Key feature	Select an appropriate method of training to develop one or more aspect of fitness (in this example, agility)

8 UNIT AND COURSE ASSESSMENT EXAMPLES

Outcome Questions

Key Concept 1

Explain the information about your performance you obtained from the study of this Key Concept.

> The main points I learned about in this key concept was that if you want to improve skill-related fitness then you need to train in specific skill-related performance contexts. Specificity is the most important part of a training programme so you need to make sure your training is specific. For example, in hockey I need to ensure that any conditioned games or practices are organised to ensure that they develop my agility. I know that practice must be specific to be useful and once you have achieved this you can then make the practice more demanding as time goes on. This is called adding overload to your training. In my case this would involve completing the practices quicker and possibly for longer as this is what I need to do to become a better player. Information about the training principle of specificity is useful. The reference to how specificity links to performance in hockey is quite well made.

Information about the training principle of specificity is useful. The reference to how specificity links to performance in hockey is quite well made.

Discuss how you applied this information when designing a relevant development programme.

> I worked on my agility with a series of maze-type runs. I performed these as sets of sprints as well as occasionally performing them with hockey dribbles. I set up my training on a circuit of exercises of different levels of difficulty. The idea of the maze runs and the hockey dribbles was that they matched the demands of dribbling in a game. Therefore, they could be considered to be specific to my needs. We moved around the circuit twice. This was good as it seemed that we got the benefit of the practice, but not too much of the same thing that we got bored. It meant as well that my heart rate was always quite high. This would also help me on the endurance side of things as well.

Training is relevant to skill-related fitness as is mention of training for a suitable amount of time.

Key Concept 2

Explain the information about your performance you obtained from the study of this Key Concept.

> Knowing that I had to make my training specific, I then went on to learn that there were two different ways to achieve this. I could either complete training on its own outside of the activity or by conditioning, which involved training through practices which link to the activity. I found out that both forms of training can be effective and that it depends on what your needs are which method of training you select. My practices were a conditioning approach, as I was actually dribbling the ball some of the time as well as trying to run quicker and more often. If I was only sprinting, for example, then this would have been training outside of the activity. However, the agility practice I was completing had a skill part to it as well as I was dribbling the ball. This helped make the training more realistic.

A grasp of the two most common types of practice is evident. This helps show evidence of the need to make any practice meaningful and realistic.

Discuss how you applied this information when designing a relevant development programme.

> I made up a six item circuit with two of the exercises being about agility. One was a diagonal maze run like sprint and the other was the same type of sprint over the same distance but dribbling the hockey ball at the same time. The practices were 1 and 4 in the circuit to allow me to link these practices with other types of quite demanding fitness exercises in hockey.
>
> The layout of the cones meant that I often had to change directly quickly and keep close control over the ball when moving at speed. The maze run involved a short 12m sprint. I made sure that I mixed up the agility exercises within a larger fitness circuit so that I was not always practising the same type of thing and always using the same type of muscles. If I had done this I would have become tired more quickly. With tasks involving different muscle groups you were able to have some rest intervals in your training and keep practising for longer. This was good as it meant that I trained for about the same time as a game of hockey lasted.

Some evidence of specific practices is described. The idea of where to place practices in a circuit which have the same type of demand is well made.

Explain the training method you used and explain why you consider it was appropriate.

> I think that this training method was useful as it was very specific to my exact agility needs. I think that if I had tried to achieve the same amount of practice benefit by either just running or playing games then this would not have happened. It was better to try and specifically practise on my weaknesses, but in a way that is realistic to my position in hockey and to my performance when I'm playing games of hockey.
>
> I think circuit training was a useful practice method as the multi-stage circuit could include a good balance of some exercises which related to hockey in general and some specific exercises for agility.

Some further information about specificity has added to the depth of explanation. More detail on the merits of using circuit training would have been useful.

Explain the programme of work you designed to develop the selected aspect of performance.

> After a warm-up, I performed a series of maze-type runs – these were 12m each way. The cones were about 1m out to each side. This meant that I would need to move 2m across when going forward, cutting across from side to side. I had to make sure I pushed off my outside foot to stay in balance when moving. This would help save time as well as keeping me in a better balanced position when running. I would go once up and round, then back, then rest. This would take about 8 secs on average for the running only exercise. Then I would rest for 12 secs and then go to the next station. The exercise in the circuit where I dribbled the hockey ball as well took a lot more time and varied more depending upon whether the ball went out to the side or not, or whether I lost control of it when at the top when turning. We moved between exercises every 30 secs and moved on at 20 secs. Mostly, this was when I was just arriving back at the start position.

Some useful detail about the practices that made up the plan of action is described.

Outcome 3: Monitor a Suitable Programme of Work

PC (a) A relevant programme of work to meet identified needs is completed

PC (b) The content of the programme of work is monitored

PC (c) Performance development is monitored

To complete the next stage of the assignment you complete a programme of work. You explain how it was useful and how you monitored progress. Your programme should be long enough and demanding enough for you to gain the information necessary to discuss your performance

Using a short table to keep a record of training diary/log of your completed training can be useful.
See the example below:

Session	Brief reflections/evaluations on or about training
1	Week 2 – Monday. A good session. Gentle warm up appeared to help. The agility exercises were I thought quite demanding. especially the second time through the circuit.
2	Week 3 – Wednesday. I think that now is the time to add some more demand to the circuit. I think this because I feel that I am not working as hard as I was before. At the end tonight. I did not have to rest up for a few minutes before getting changed as I have done in previous training sessions.
3	Week 4 – The extra agility dribble that I have included has worked well. It makes the amount of specific exercise I do that bit more. but all in all I think this is a good idea for my training.

Explain how and why some parts of the programme were adapted as the programme progressed, or why you left the programme unchanged.

The main part of the programme remained unchanged for the first few weeks with my 2 repetitions of 6 exercises built into my overall training session at which we also took part in practice games. After week 3 though I swapped the long hit and jog exercise in my circuit and replaced it with another agility hockey dribble. I switched the circuit around so that I did the agility run and hockey dribble as exercise number 1. 3 and 5 to keep them apart from the other exercises. I thought that this would be better as it would keep me practising the area of performance I most need to practise and I thought as the weeks went on that I could cope with the extra demand. The times I took for the running exercise show that this was the case.

> Useful suggestions for adding to the specificity of training through adapting circuit.

Explain how you monitored the effect of your training programme.

> I used time as the main way of working out whether my training was effective or not. For the single agility run my running speed was about 8 seconds and my rest was 12 seconds. I had a partner time my run to make sure that I kept up with this running time and that I did not get any slower.
>
> I used time as well for the hockey dribble but this worked less well. This is because the time taken was less accurate. This is because sometimes you would lose control of the ball and this could add a lot of time to the time taken. I sorted this by trying to work out my average time from the 2 repetitions of the circuit. My target time was 20 seconds. Doing this was a help as it reduced the effect of having one poor exercise in the circuit.

Knowledge of results through monitoring time taken for exercises was useful evaluating training exercise effectiveness.

Outcome 4: Review the Analysis and Development Process

PC (a)   The effectiveness of the analysis and development process is explained

PC (b)   The effects on performance are explained

PC (c)   Future development needs are described

To complete the final stage of your assignment you need to reflect on the effectiveness of the programme and explain any future development needs.

Explain the effect that the analysis and development process had on the selected aspect of performance.

> My teacher always says 'There's only one way. We'll know whether your training programme worked when we get back to the game.' So this is what happened. The idea was to play more games after my weeks of working on my agility and see if I was a bit quicker.
>
> The results showed that I had improved. I was better at getting away with the ball from other players. However, this was against generally poorer teams so this might have affected things. I still felt that I was moving a lot better and, crucially, that I was able to keep my balance a bit better when moving at top speed and not look awkward. This helped me keep better control of the ball. The next task is to check on my hockey dribbling and running when playing against better teams and whether I can keep this going all the way through the game, as I also need to work on this as well.

The link to skill-related fitness is continued and this adds to the relevance of the analysis completed.

Explain the effect that the analysis and development process had on your overall performance.

> I think that having more control over the ball when dribbling has helped my overall performance. Being able to move a bit quicker away from defenders has allowed me to choose easier passing options. For example, if I can get past the defender and into space then you have a clearer passing channel whereas if the defender is close to you and you cannot dribble quickly away from them this makes your overall performance more difficult.

Useful linking of the benefits of training to increased effectiveness within role in hockey team.

Discuss your future development needs in this area of performance.

> Now that my control and agility has improved as well as my ability to keep going all through the game. I think there is still a need to keep working on my basic running speed. I'm not the quickest and I think that if I can keep doing some sprint training then at least it will help me make the best of what I have got. So. this is what I think I need to do in the future. I need to work on a physical aspect of speed now that my skill-related aspect of fitness (agility) has got better.

Some reference and link to other aspects of fitness.

Tip: When explaining the effects on performance, remind yourself of what the 'Performance Outcome' in Higher Still Physical Education mentions. It looks at 'demonstrate effective performance in challenging contexts'. It mentions, in particular, the importance of 'a broad performance repertoire', 'appropriate decisions' and 'control and fluency'. Try to link your answer to these criteria when answering Outcome 4 on 'Review the analysis and development process'.

Unit Summary: *This is a mostly coherent Unit answer which is at the Unit pass standard. There is some evidence of work above the minimum standard. The thread of the answer is quite well retained, as is the ink between training and performance.*

Unit Assessment: Skills and Techniques (Higher)

Your Unit assignment takes you through different analysis stages. The Cycle of Analysis is one popular approach. See diagram 2 on page 11.

You begin your assignment by selecting the activity, area of Analysis of Performance and specific aspect of performance you will be trying to improve.

Activity: Hockey **Area of Analysis of Performance**: Skills and Techniques

Specific aspect of performance analysed: Passing improvement through opposed/unopposed practices and conditioned, small-sided/coached games.

You then briefly explain the significance of this aspect to your whole performance.

> As an attacker, I have noticed from past games that my passing appears to be weak at times. This limits the effectiveness of my performance and the performance of my team. This is mostly because poor passing can limit our team's attacking options. Passing in attack, even over short distances, is always likely to be difficult as the defenders are likely to be working to their maximum to try and defend at this point.

You then need to begin the **Investigation** process through collecting information about your performance. There are a number of methods of collecting information which might be useful for you to consider. Many of these are outlined on pages 14 to 20. Refer to these when choosing the best method for your investigation.

In this example, game analysis sheets have been used for both the initial and focused levels of data collection.

Initial Level of Data Collection

I had the following game analysis sheet completed. This allowed me to find out about my skills in a seven-a-side hockey game lasting 30 minutes each half.

Game Analysis Sheet

Team: Scotstown Academy **Role**: Attacker
Opposition: Central High School **Date**: 25/11/05

✓ = effective   ✗ = ineffective

Time (minutes)	Control (first touch)	Passing (under 10m)	Passing (over 10m)	Dribbling	Tackling	Shooting
1st half 0–10	✓✓	✓		✓	✓	
11–19	✓✗	✗✓✓	✗✓	✗	✓✗	✓
21–30	✓	✓✗	✓	✓✗	✓	✗
2nd half 0–10	✓✓✓	✓✓✗✗			✓	✓
11–19	✓✓	✓✓✗✗	✗✓			✗
21–30	✗✗✓✓	✗✓✗✗	✓	✗		

Unit Assessment: Skills and Techniques (Higher)

Personal review

I analysed these results after the game. This allowed me to obtain feedback about my performance. I could see that for most of the game I contributed to our attack by performing my skills quite consistently. However, it appeared that my short passing was the poorest part of my game. This was as I expected it to be. It limited our attacking options. I felt very comfortable and had no problems lasting the 60 minutes. I decided to focus specifically on my short passing to see if I could find out more information.

Focused Level of Data Collection

I had the following game analysis sheet completed. This allowed me to find out about my passing under pressure when passing in a seven-a-side hockey game lasting 30 minutes each half.

Game Analysis Sheet

Team: Scotstown Academy
Opposition: Central High School

Role: Attacker
Date: 25/11/05

✓ = effective   ✗ = ineffective

Time (minutes)	Pass forward under pressure	Pass forward under less pressure	Pass to side or back under pressure	Pass to side or back under little pressure
1st half 0–10	✓✓ ✗ ✗ ✗	✓	✓	✓✓
11–19	✓ ✗ ✗	✓✓	✓✓	✓
21–30	✗ ✗	✗ ✓	✗ ✗	✗
2nd half 0–10	✓		✓	✓✓✓
11–19	✓ ✗ ✗	✓✓	✓	✓ ✗
21–30	✗ ✓ ✗	✓ ✗	✓ ✗ ✗	✓

Personal review

The quantifiable evidence obtained from my movement analysis data confirmed my initial feelings that my occasionally unsatisfactory performance was due to poor passing under pressure. I was working hard as part of my team and I made lots of runs but, when under pressure, my passing was going astray. Most of my poor passes were overhit.

Remember: With your Unit Assessments you are able to directly use the data that you have collected in the answering of your question. The answers to Outcomes 1-4 (pages 123 to 131) are based on the data collected on the game analysis sheets above.

Outcome 1: Analyse Performance in an Activity

- PC (a) Methods selected and used for observing and recording data are valid

- PC (b) Data gathered are valid

- PC (c) Performance strengths and weaknesses are analysed

- PC (d) Development needs are analysed

Outcome questions

Explain the main information you collected from the data.

Student example answer

Teacher example comment

The initial data confirmed that it was my passing that was the most limited part of my game. It highlighted that my passing effectiveness was only at 50% for my short passing of less than 10 metres. Even though the pitch was quite small and that as an attacker I was closely marked this is still a low success rate. I made 16 passes during the 30 minute game and only half of the passes were effective. Other areas of my game like control were better. The initial data indicated that I controlled the ball with a good first touch on 11 out of 14 occasions. This indicates that getting the ball under control when 'on the deck' was not so much of a problem.

The focused data indicates that the major weakness was my passing under pressure. When defenders were close to me I tended to sometimes overhit passes almost as if I was panicking a little. The rest of my game was better and my effort as part of the team was well commented upon. What I needed though was a greater degree of accuracy in the timing and weight of pass when my team was attacking in the crucial last third of the pitch.

A useful outline explanation is provided which draws upon information collected from both the initial and focused data.

Explain why the methods you used to record data were valid.

I wanted the data to highlight how effectively I played in my role as a striker. The initial data showed what I suspected, namely that it was my passing that let me down the most. My other main striking skills were better. The initial data was appropriate because it looked at my whole game. The other thing that was good about it is that information was collected about both my first half and my second half performances. It was also clearly set out and easy to use. When I was observed carrying out certain skills by my classmates, my performances could be noted down.

To allow further depth of analysis, I used a detailed analysis sheet to collect my focused data. This data highlighted my effectiveness at passing both under pressure from defenders and when under less pressure. The method was reliable and easy to use, and allowed to me plan my later training programme. The criteria were also specific to the problem I had identified.

The development of data that was specific to passing under pressure was useful and appropriate for Higher Level work.

UNIT AND COURSE ASSESSMENT EXAMPLES

Analyse how your data helped you recognise your performance strengths and weaknesses.

The results showed that my performance broke down slightly when I was under pressure. Passing is tricky under pressure. Players need to think about timing. weight and accuracy of pass. These are the most important things. My results showed that my timing. weight and accuracy broke down a bit when I was under pressure. I made only 6 effective penetrative forward passes when under pressure but II ineffective ones.

The data showed that I rarely made mistakes when under little pressure. My impression was that I overhit my passes when I was under pressure. I think I rushed things a bit and felt that if I give the ball a good hit then the pass would at least 'get there.' However. my other attackers often could not control the pass and the ball went on past them. Often they gave me a 'cold' look as well. This let me know that I'd hit the ball too hard again. My teacher said that it was good that I could recognise this look from my team-mates. Feedback is very important in skill learning. However. possession is important in hockey and with the other teams being able to counter attack so quickly playing better passes was required.

> Relevant knowledge about passing is apparent (timing, weight, accuracy) as is the link between this content knowledge and the student's own performance in a game of hockey.

Analyse how your data helped you recognise your development needs.

The data was very useful as it was specific to my performance. The data was relevant to the position I play in hockey and it was obtained against players of my own level of ability. Because of this accurate record of how I performed. I now feel that I am better prepared to design a relevant training programme. which is based on the exact parts of my overall game which require the most immediate attention. Moving from initial to focused data was useful as it helped move from something which I thought as a hunch was a problem to more detailed focus level data which highlight the specifics of the main part of my game which would benefit from improvement.

> Clear link established between accurate data and development needs.

Outcome 2: Use Knowledge and Understanding to Analyse Performance

- PC (a) Relevant Key Concepts and key features are selected and used to analyse performance in detail

- PC (b) Relevant information sources are used effectively to plan performance development

- PC (c) A programme of work is designed to effectively address identified needs

To complete this next stage of the assignment you need to link your data to relevant Key Concepts. This will help you to analyse your performance and plan a development programme. Each assignment answer requires to link to two Key Concepts. You might find it useful to specify the key features you are using to help your analyse as well.

Key Concept 1	The concept of skill and skilled performance
Key feature	How skills and techniques are performed for effective consistent performance whilst also displaying qualities of control, fluency and economy of movement
Key Concept 2	The development of skill and the refinement of technique
Key feature	Methods of practice – opposed/unopposed and conditioned /small-sided and coached games

Outcome questions

Key Concept 1

Explain the information about your performance you obtained from the study of this Key Concept.

As my weakness was overhitting passes. I needed to look at ways of playing short, accurate passes, which were hit just right when I was under pressure. What my passing required in order to be more effective was to make more controlled fluent passes where the right degree of effort was used, but which were played when I was in a tight situation where I was being marked. In a basic sense my passing was accurate but when passing under pressure the skill of passing is more complex and my performance level went down.

The information from the data tended to suggest that when I saw the passing chance open up that I tended to hit the ball hard with the thinking being that this was the best way to get the ball through the gap. However, a hockey ball is both hard to stop and control for my team-mates and it is also quite difficult to intercept at times. Therefore, it would be much better and more skilled and effective if I played the ball with the correct weighting and timing. In doing this I gave my team-mates a pass they could possibly continue the attack with. It would also add to my performance, if I could pass with the correct degree of effort and accuracy, as part of being a skilled hockey player is good stickwork with the necessary backlift and follow through. At present, I am taking too big a backswing and follow through than is necessary for a short pass.

> Information about the concept of skilled performance in hockey is evident through reference to how control, fluency and economy of movement are required in hockey passing.

Discuss, in detail, how you applied this information when designing a relevant development programme.

> The first thing I had to do was organise game-related practices that would be specifically useful to me.
>
> I made sure that my skills training programme was effective. To do this, I took into account my specific needs. These were
>
> * playing passes quickly
> * playing passes at the right time
> * using the correct weight in passing
> * being accurate in my passing
> * using economic movements (no excessive backlift or follow through)
>
> Therefore, my knowledge of skilled performance was helpful in that it showed me that if you want to be better at short passing in a game then your training needs to involve some degree of active opposition. This reflects the fact that I needed to practise my passing by treating it as a complex skill and not a basic skill where there were no defenders involved.
>
> I also required to consider my passing in attack in hockey as an open skill as it takes place during competitive play when there is direct competitive play and where you cannot be control of the situation. For example, the defenders can move in unpredictable ways, which means that you also require to pay close attention to a range of different factors and adapt to what is happening in active situations.

Relevant knowledge about effective passing as part of skilled performance is evident. References to passing in hockey demands as open and complex skill are helpful for showing grasp of important factors which would influence design of training programme.

Key Concept 2

Explain the information about your performance you obtained from the study of this Key Concept.

> On my course we have looked at a number of methods of practice. The key consideration is to make sure that you match the correct practice with the different skills and techniques you are trying to improve. Getting this connection correct is critical for making practice useful. One of the things which we learned about early on in our course is that inappropriate practice is futile.
>
> What I was attempting to do with my passing was consolidate and make better a skill which I already knew about and could complete. What was required was the refinement of the skill rather than learning it from the beginning. This affects the method of practice that I choose. I needed a practice which was demanding and matched the demands of hockey games. From the range of practice methods that we have worked on during our course the best ones to use were opposed/unopposed and conditioned/small-sided game practices.

A grasp of two relevant forms of practice and how they link to the performance demands associated with hockey is evident.

Discuss, in detail, how you applied this information when designing a relevant development programme.

I next considered the specific practices I would work on and how I could make these more demanding as time went on. To avoid boredom and keeping my passing standard at the same level, I had to make sure that my practices replicated the demands of a game. This meant that after a warm up that we would spend say 20 minutes on opposed practices in boxes and small-sided conditioned games, before ending with a more competitive game.

The other thing I worked out was how long I would work for within the box practices. A few short practices are better than a session which is too long and so you might become bored and tired. I would work for a small burst of, say, 3 minutes, then rest, recover and practise again.

The opposed practices I worked on were completed in 10m boxes. In these boxes, I used opponents to make me feel under pressure. I also made some of the practices more demanding by making sure that I had to take a first touch and then play the pass immediately. By adding difficulty like this, I was increasing the intensity of the practices. Taking a few touches and then turning around and looking are easier than playing the ball after one touch. The good think about small box work in hockey is that you can very easily add or take away the level of opposition. It is very important that the practice is challenging and achievable, but yet realistic and possible to do.

I also combined these practices with other skill practices so that my whole set of practices covered all areas of the game but, in my case, had a particular emphasis on passing under pressure. The other feature of my training was that during this time I was also involved in playing small-sided games and conditioned games. We spent about 10 minutes of the 20 minutes training having conditioned and small-sided games.

> The specific development of the opposed practices and conditioned games is quite carefully explained with suitable attention to detail.

> The emphasis on box passing practices within a larger hockey training programme is a valid point well made.

Analyse the training method you used and explain why you consider it was appropriate.

I think the main benefit of the training methods adopted was that active opposition was involved in both methods of practice. In the box practices with active opposition the 'rules' of the practice was that if the defenders gained possession of the ball then they switched and became attackers. This helped make the practice realistic for them. If it was the case that they had to defend for a few minutes then swap it is easy to predict that they would switch off from the practice and just move around and wait till they got their turn as attackers. For skills which are open and complex opposition is very useful. If it was possible to show control and fluency when practising then the practice transfer to full games would likely be higher.

The other addition of having this type of box practice and small-sided games was that the practice of skills was continuous as the practice and game just kept going for quite a few minutes. This was good as it kept everyone on task and also reflected the type of game which hockey is, where play is continuous and everyone knows what to do at short corners and at free hits.

> The reference to 'open', 'complex' and 'continuous' indicates that there is a clear understanding of effective practice linking with effective performance.

Analyse the programme of work you designed to develop the selected aspect of performance.

> Overall, I do think that the practices adopted were effective as they clearly linked to my specific skill needs and my current ability level. The key consideration was to ensure that the practice was quality practice with the right degree of demand and that the amount of time spent on practice went on for a relatively short but suitable amount of time.
>
> The reason why practice was short was that it was quite high in intensity. When in the boxes and games you had to be 'switched on' to all that was happening as there could be sudden changes as some passes went astray and as some interceptions were made. A high level of attention is required in open and complex practice settings.

> The reasons provided to support the design of the training programme are quite well explained.

Outcome 3: Monitor a Programme of Work

- PC (a) A relevant programme of work to address identified needs is completed

- PC (b) The content and demand of the programme of work is monitored

- PC (c) Performance development is monitored effectively

To complete the next stage of the assignment you complete a programme of work. You explain how it was useful and how you monitored progress. Your programme should be long enough and demanding enough for you to gain the information necessary to discuss your performance

Using a short table to keep a record of training diary/log of your completed training can be useful. See the example below.

Session	Brief reflections/evaluations on or about training
1	Week 1 – Monday. Good warm up, pitch in good condition. After stretching started in 4v1 box which was quite good. Encouraged to play and move so that we avoided holding the same place in the square. This made the practice a bit better and more realistic as it involved turning and calling for the ball as we moved across the square.
2	Week 2 – Wednesday. Moved to 3v1 in the passing practices in the 10m box. This is necessary as having to three players to hit to is too many. If your team-mates move to the full width of the box then the one defender is really stretched. What I found with this practice was that I had to be more accurate with the pass as it would travel closer to the defender. This was good as it was exactly what I needed to be practising.
3	Week 4 – Monday. We have moved to 3v1 playing a single touch to control and then passing when it was on. I often used something just like using a slap shot, so that there was little time spent on the preparation of the pass, time which the defenders could use to their advantage and close you down.

Explain how and why some parts of the programme were adapted as the programme progressed, or why you left the programme unchanged.

As I mentioned earlier, after the warm up I move to complete a programme of opposed practices in boxes that were designed to be realistic to the demands of a larger game of hockey. This part of the session lasted around 20 minutes with only around 3 minutes being spent on any one box practice. The remainder of the 20 minutes was spent on other skill practices such as shooting, corner drills and tackling. We trained twice a week — Monday and Wednesday.

Step 1 involved us playing 4v1 in a box. We swapped in if our pass was poor. Play continued for a few minutes. I had to work on drawing the defender and, when the time was right, passing the ball accurately and at the right speed. This was my big concern.

In the next practice the method moved to 3v1. This meant that the level of opposition had increased as there were now only two other attackers to pass to. This was Step 2. Again, this practice lasted for a few minutes. This time, the task was more demanding, because the timing of passes was more important. Because the defender knew that there were only two others to pass to, it was easier for him or her to cover the passes. This occasionally resulted in me giving the ball a real belt. However, this practice was about keeping my control and passing the ball in time, without hitting it too hard and passing it to suit a shorter like setting.

Step 3 was also 3v1 but we were only able to take a single touch before passing. Again, this made the practice more difficult as I had even less time to pass. I had to prepare more quickly as the defender knew I had to play the ball. As the weeks went on, I moved between these steps as part of my circuits. I spent weeks 1 and 2 on Step 1, moving to Step 3 in weeks 4 and 5. Moving to the next level of opposition was not automatic. It was dependent upon the skill level which was evident in our practice.

This same idea was applied in the small-sided conditioned games that we played. Our teacher informed us that we would move on to make practice ever more like 'games' as it became evident that we could adapt to the new demands we were faced with. At the outset, the attacking team had an advantage in practice in that they had two additional players. This was reduced to one and then removed altogether in our small-sided games.

Some relevant details about the practices are noted.

Some useful further details on how practices functioned, particularly with regard to when and why the student moved on to the next practice stage is useful in explaining how the level of opposition was increased.

Slightly greater detail on why the small game part of the programme was adapted, was required.

Explain how you monitored the effect of your training programme.

> One of the main ways in which the opposition practices were monitored was to study closely the effort levels of the defenders. If their effort level lowered this could be because they were either too tired or because they were giving up because they did not realistically consider that they could actually get possession of the ball. When this happens it is often time to balance the practice up by making it harder for the attackers and this is what we did by increasing the difficulty for them.
>
> The same was true, but to a lesser extent, in the conditioned games where for some reason the defenders appear to try hard at all times. Again, I think the fact that if you gained possession of the ball that you instantly became an attacker was a significant reason.

Some relevant points about how to monitor performance are explained.

Outcome 4: Evaluate the Analysis and Development Process

- PC (a) The effectiveness of the analysis and development process is discussed

- PC (b) The effects on performance are discussed

- PC (c) Future development needs are discussed

To complete the final stage of your assignment you need to reflect on the effectiveness of the programme and discuss any future development needs.

Discuss the effect that the analysis and development process had on the selected aspect of performance.

> These practices definitely helped me. I began to notice that I had become better at playing a slap shot type pass. This involved me hitting the ball with one hand at the top and one halfway down the stick, a bit like an ice hockey player would. Passing like this gave me more time and control and also meant that I did not hit the ball too hard. When I had both hands at the top of the stick I used to hit the ball to hard. This slap technique worked better as I got used to it in practice, which proves that practice is a good idea. It is also a good hitting technique as it is quite economic in that I did not swing the hockey stick too much. It also gave me a bit more time to look at the positioning of the defenders and make decisions based on where they were positioned.

A relevant explanation about the effects of improved passing technique is discussed.

Discuss the effect that the analysis and development process had on your overall performance.

> The new hitting technique has had a beneficial effect on my performance. This is evident in the accuracy and weighting of my passing in attack. In the weeks ahead I intend to complete further assessments to confirm whether this is the case when the facts are examined. However, from my reflections about my performance in games it does appear better. One benefit from the box practices was that it also helped me to improve my stickwork in preparing to pass. In the 3v1 box this had to be completed quickly in case the defender closed down on you. Improving this aspect of performance as the basis for beginning an effective pass has been useful.
>
> In games, one of the things I now concentrate on is trying to relax and pass the ball with the correct weight and timing after drawing the defender and committing them to trying to tackle. Achieving this enables my attackers to keep the attack going rather than running to retrieve the ball. Being more confident in my passing enables me to panic less when defenders begin closing me down.

Some relevant reporting about the effects of improved passing technique had on overall performance are discussed.

Discuss your future development needs in this area of performance.

> I consider that the best way to evaluate my performance and use this evidence to inform my future development needs would be to complete further similar games of hockey and record my progress against the criteria that were used for my first assessments. This would ensure that the baseline information I used at the beginning is used for later comparisons. This would give accuracy to my end-of-programme findings and provide further information about whether it was the same passing part of my game which required attention or whether it was now another aspect of performance which now required attention and training.

Brief relevant evaluation comments are provided.

Tip: When explaining the effects on performance, remind yourself of what the 'Performance Outcome' in Higher Still Physical Education mentions. It looks at 'demonstrate effective performance in challenging contexts'. It mentions, in particular, the importance of 'a broad performance repertoire', 'appropriate decisions' and 'control and fluency'. Try to link your answer to these criteria when answering Outcome 4 on 'Review the analysis and development process'.

Unit Summary: *This is a mostly coherent Unit answer which is at the Unit pass standard. There is some evidence of work above the minimum standard. The thread of the answer is quite well retained as is the link between training and performance.*

8 UNIT AND COURSE ASSESSMENT EXAMPLES

Course Assessment: Structures, Strategies and Composition (Intermediate 2)

(a) Choose **one** activity. Describe in detail a structure, strategy or composition you have used.   4

(b) Describe how you **collected information** about the structure, strategy or composition you have described in part (a).   4

(c) Explain the major **strengths** in the structure, strategy or composition you have described in part (a).   4

(d) Explain the major weaknesses in the structure, strategy or composition you have described in part (a).   4

(e) Describe how you evaluated the structure, strategy or composition you have described in part (a).   4

(20)

(a) Choose **one** activity. Describe in detail a structure, strategy or composition you have used.   4

The activity I have chosen is Badminton. As I have a good range of shots and am quite a skilful performer, able to use different technique to win points, I decided that the best strategy for me to use was to play a 'percentage game'.

The idea behind a percentage game is to play relatively safe shots and to focus on playing the shuttlecock to the corners of the opponent's court. By using such shots I can keep my opponent moving away from the centre of his or her court and so his or her chances of playing attacking shots will be reduced. This allows me to play what are called 'building shots'. These shots are used, as the name suggests, to build up attacks. For example, if I play a deep overhead clear to the back of my opponent's court, he or she might be able to play only a quite weak return to the middle of my court from where I would play a smash. The idea here is to only play a smash when it is relatively safe to do so (high percentage), as opposed to taking on more risky shots and making errors when doing so.

> The link between technique and strategy is well made. However, some further description about the strategy (width, depth, mobility) would have been useful.

Summary
3 out of 4 marks awarded. The answer is clear and occasionally detailed.

(b) Describe how you **collected information** about the structure, strategy or composition you have described in part (a).

4

Collecting information for this strategy was the tricky part. What I eventually decided to do after discussing it with my teacher, was to draw out a court diagram, just like the one shown below.

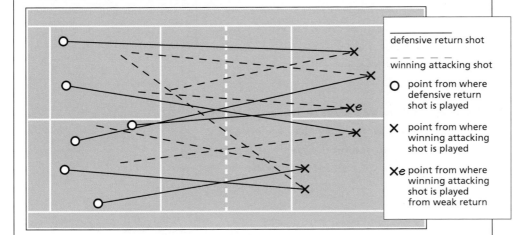

defensive return shot

– – – – –
winning attacking shot

O point from where defensive return shot is played

X point from where winning attacking shot is played

Xe point from where winning attacking shot is played from weak return

The observer marked on the court diagram from where I played the shots that lead to winning smashes. This was quite difficult for the observer to do and meant that we had to take time between points to record the details. However, this was worth doing as the examples on the diagram above show. From this data, I was able to find whether or not my building shots which lead up to smashes were helpful in winning points. This data was useful because it gave me specific information on whether or not the depth and width I was after in playing building shots to the corners was working or not.

The only difficulty with this type of data collection was what to do if my opponent played a very weak shot which allowed me to smash easily. I decided to have all my shots noted down but I made sure that my observer wrote an 'e' beside the X when a point was won from an unforced error or poor return by my opponent. This was because I really wanted to find out which points were won through my playing to my chosen strategy.

I collected data from games in which my opponents were of similar standards to me because this made my data more accurate and reliable.

The specific issues about collecting relevant data are carefully described. What separates a winning point based or strategy rather than other factors has been well thought through at the beginning.

Summary
4 marks out of 4 awarded. The student's answer is clear, full and detailed. His or her method of collecting information has been well thought through.

(c) Explain the major **strengths** in the structure, strategy or composition you have described in part (a).

4

My main strengths in this percentage game strategy were that I was able to read different situations quite quickly and play a range of shots which helped put my strategy into practice. For example, I was able to think through whether to play a low net return or a high clear to the back of the court in good time. These decisions were based on where my opponent was positioned. This improved my confidence in using the strategy. As a result, I did not force the play too much. One possible problem with this strategy is that if you try to play to the corners too much, then you can hit the shuttle out of the court and lose games through making unforced or unnecessary errors.

My main strength was that I was able to play to safe areas of the court without unforced errors such as hitting the shuttle out of the court. This was achieved mostly by hitting down the line rather than across the court. When I hit across the court, my opponent often had the chance to step across and play the shuttle away from me and win the point outright.

> The game examples of the student's strengths in action are well explained. Some further links to how these strengths linked to the strategy were required.

> **Summary**
> **2 marks out of 4 awarded. The answer uses a wide range of relevant concepts to make sound judgements.**

(d) Explain the major weaknesses in the structure, strategy or composition you have described in part (a).

4

My major weaknesses were that I was weak at hitting the shuttle across the width of the back line when hitting it to the back of the court and that I did not use deception enough.

The first weakness meant that when I was playing clears to the back of the court, I would hit them down the middle of the court too often. I was therefore not using the width of the court as well as I might have done, even though I was using the depth of the court well. This meant that my opponent could return my shots with overhead forehand shots. This is quite a strong shot whereas an overhead backhand shot is weaker. What I needed to do more was to play the shuttle over to the back of the court on my opponent's backhand side so that I could force him or her into playing a weaker overhead backhand return. The results of playing better building shots were that it was easier for me to play winning shots from them.

My other weakness was that I did not manage to use deception enough. Often it is pretty clear to my opponent what type of shot I am going to play and where I am about to play it too. This means that my play is rather predictable and that at times my opponent can play attacking shots from my building shots.

> The game examples of the student's weaknesses in action are well explained. On this occasion there are some better links to how these weaknesses related to the strategy.

> **Summary**
> **3 marks out of 4 awarded. The student has used a range of relevant concepts to make sound judgements.**

(e) Describe how you evaluated the structure, strategy or composition you have described in part (a).

4

For my evaluation, it was important to me to compare how well I had done at the end of the season in comparison with how well I had done at the beginning. This would allow me to see whether or not I had improved. For this reason, I decided to evaluate my performance again by completing a further observation schedule that used the same court details as used on the first occasion. I ensured that my re-observation was recorded during a game against a player of similar ability, and in the same type of singles competitive game, as when my initial observation was recorded. This ensured my results were accurate and useful to my evaluation. It allowed me to compare my later information, following my training programme, against my baseline information from before my training programme. I wanted to see whether more of my winning smashes resulted from playing building shots that were deeper or wider than before, while still being high percentage shots because I had managed to avoid hitting them out of the court.

The evaluation of performance is well explained. Again, a clearer link to the strategy being followed would have helped the quality of the evaluation explanation.

Summary
3 marks out of 4 awarded. The student's answer contains a clear and full description of the evaluation process.

Total: 15 marks out of 20 awarded.

KEY WORDS CHECKLIST

It is important that you have a good working vocabulary of words and their meanings. Check that you are familiar with the meanings of the words below, which relate to the different key concepts

Performance Appreciation

Key Concepts	Pages	Key words
Overall nature and demands of quality performance	22	'experiential' 'precision' 'control' 'accuracy'
Technical, physical, personal and special qualities of performance	23-26	'emotional control' 'codes of conduct' 'imagination' 'flair' 'creativity'
Mental factors influencing performance	27-28	'motivation' 'managing stress' 'self-confidence' 'comfort zone' 'visualisation'
The use of appropriate models of performance	29-30	'personal style' 'mental imagery'
Planning and managing personal performance improvement	31-32	'on-going monitoring of performance' 'setting performance goals'

Preparation of the Body

Key Concepts	Pages	Key words
Fitness assessment in relation to personal performance and the demands of activities standardised procedures'	34-37	'regular monitoring of performance' 'test norms'
Application of different types of fitness in the development of activity specific performance	38-39	'performance review' 'conditioning training'
Physical, skill-related and mental aspects of fitness	40-45	'speed endurance' 'strength endurance' 'dynamic strength' 'local muscular endurance' 'flexibility' 'reaction time' 'agility' 'balance' 'movement anticipation' 'co-ordination' level of arousal' 'rehearsal' 'managing your emotions'
Principles and methods of training	46-52	'specificity' 'progressive overload' 'intensity' 'duration' 'frequency' 'combined skill and fitness training programmes' 'adaptation' 'reversibility'
Planning, implementing and monitoring training	53-56	'identifiable goals' 'short and long term goals' 'periodisation' 'peaking for performance' 'tapering down' 'phases of training' 'training cycles' 'monitoring performance'

Skills and Techniques

Key Concepts	Pages	Key words
The concepts of skill and skilled performance	58-62	'fluent controlled movements' 'selecting correct options' 'skills which reflect experience and ability' 'information processing' 'learning loop' 'decision-making' 'open and closed skills' 'simple and complex skills' discrete / serial and continuous skills' 'variations in technique'
Skill/technique improvement through mechanical analysis or movement analysis or consideration of quality	63-66	'force' 'body levers' 'planes of movement' 'preparation, action and recovery' 'managing effort factors in performance' 'personal and technical qualities'
The development of skill and the refinement of technique	67-78	'preparation, practice and automatic stages of learning' 'solo/shadow/partner/group practice' 'opposed/unopposed practice' 'repetition/drills practice' 'massed/distributed practice' 'conditioned games/small sided games' 'whole/part/whole practice' ' work to rest ratios' 'progression' 'internal motivation' 'goal setting' 'external motivation' 'concentration' 'forms of feedback' 'knowledge of results' 'effect of boredom and fatigue'

Structures, Strategies and Composition

Key Concepts	Pages	Key words
The structures, strategies and /or compositional elements that are fundamental to activities	80	'tempo' 'deception' 'design form and style with a composition'
Identification of strengths and weaknesses in performance in terms of - roles and relationships, formations, tactical or design elements and choreography	81-88	'support' 'continuity' 'pressure' 'improvisation' 'cohesion' 'width' 'depth' 'mobility' 'systems of play' 'positive team/group ethos' 'interpreting stimulus' 'timing' 'improvisation'
Information processing, problem-solving and decision-making when working to develop and improve performance	89-92	'adapting and refining' 'individual and group decision-making' 'dynamics and relationships' 'effective decision-making under pressure'

Remember that these are example answers or explanations of the type of answers you should give. Your own answers will be based on **your** experiences of **your** activities. Check with your teacher how good your answers are.

Area 1: Performance Appreciation (see questions on pages 32-33)

1. Performance in different activities will vary with regard to the experiential nature of performance, the special challenges of performance and the quality focus required within activities.

2. • type of activity – individual, team or group
    • different skills and technique required
    • the rules and codes of conduct required
    • the scoring system required

3. **Hockey, Attacker**

    Physical quality: Speed endurance – the ability to make regular sprints throughout the game

    Technical quality: Accuracy and precision when passing and shooting

    Personal quality: Ability to work well as part of a team

    Special quality: Can be inventive in beating defenders in attack though flair and deception

4. It could be evident through your:
    • maintaining you level of motivation and concentration
    • performing within the accepted rules and codes of conduct within the activity
    • controlling your aggression
    • effectively communicating within your team/group.

5. Visualising, touching and hearing are three senses you can use to help you develop imagery

6. Begin by finding a quiet place and lie down in a comfortable position with your eyes closed. Breathe in a steady deep rhythm through your nose and become aware of your breathing. Continue for a few minutes. When you finish, lie quietly for a further few minutes, closed eyes at first then with opened eyes. If your mind wanders try to relax again through concentrating on your breathing rhythm.

7. • It provides you with a useful reference point for performance comparison, most often at the beginning and end of your planned training programme.
    • It helps you to determine training priorities.
    • You can study the fine detail of the model performer to learn about the different skills and technique they use.

8. They are useful as goal achievement strategies for achieving longer-term goals

9. • **Specific**: goals should be specific to your ability and experience
    • **Measurable**: goals should be capable of being measured in order to estimate level of improvement
    • **Realistic**: goals should be challenging but achievable in order to sustain your motivation
    • **Recorded**: goals should be recorded in order to allow meaningful evaluation of performance improvement to occur

10. **Activity: Table tennis**

Quality performance	Reason
Commitment	1 Try to return every shot 2 Make careful shot selection – avoid being over ambitious
Concentration	1 Can selectively attend to the most important influences on performance 2 Can maintain attention throughout game and avoid being easily distracted
Composure	1 Keep calm. Avoid becoming upset by unpredictable circumstances, such as a shot that clips the side of the table. 2 Pause between service points to take time to remain calm.
Confidence	1 Play full repertoire of shots including difficult complex ones 2 Can remain focused and positive even if a run of a few points is lost.

11.

Factor	Objectives for improvement	Methods of achieving objectives
Self confidence	Self talk	Positive thoughts before performance
	Task goals	Goals which focus on your own personal improvement
	Structured competition	Performing against carefully chosen performers/teams where an effective performance is demanding but achievable
Level of anxiety and and arousal	Level of readiness for activity	Consideration of individual levels of arousal and anxiety within activities
		Consciously trying to relax mind and muscles prior to performance
		Structured warm up using motivational 'tools': music, self talk, etc.
Concentration	Selective attention	Consideration of the focus of attention, broad / narrow focus.
	Task demands	Practising concentration over time, practising shifting the focus of attention and refocusing.

Area 2: Preparation of the Body (see questions on pages 56-57)

1.
   - It allows you to obtain baseline fitness information that is specific to you
   - It allows you to compare your performance on an ongoing basis during your training programme
   - You can compare yourself with other performers through reviewing your fitness assessment results on standardised tests
   - It allows you to base your improvement programme on both objective accurate results as well as subjective thoughts and reflections

2. The Harvard step test is one effective method of testing aerobic capacity. The aim is to use your recovery rate from a standardised test procedure and test calculation to measure your own specific aerobic fitness level.

3. Objectives that are specific to your existing practical ability, your role within an activity and in line with your individual/team training goals.

4.
   - It develops physical, skill-related and mental aspects of fitness at the same time
   - It is specific to the activity being followed
   - The level of demand can match those required in the activity. For example in swimming conditioning training would involve the use of the specific and patterns of breathing that were required in swimming competitions.

5. a. 'Speed endurance' is the ability to perform a series of short sprints repeatedly over a relatively long period. For example, a football wing back will be expected to sprint to support attacks and defence throughout the entire 90-minute game. '

   b. Strength endurance' is the ability to perform a series of strong movements over a relatively long period. For example, forwards in rugby union will be expected to push against their opponents in a scrum throughout the entire 80 minute game.

6. **Swimming**

   During a 200 m individual medley, my opponent moved ahead of me during the third (breaststroke) leg. I knew that I was performing at my best and that I had my fastest stoke (front crawl) to come next in the freestyle final leg. As a result, I was able to control my emotions by carefully considering my speed. I was able to gradually move back into a winning position, rather than being rushed into trying to catch my opponent immediately. This might have proved too tiring and so ineffective.

7. anaerobic ⟷ 4   1   5   2   3 aerobic

8. Example answer: 'strength' 'co-ordination' 'use of mental rehearsal'

   Javelin (athletics)

   In javelin, I need explosive strength to generate distance in the throw. Co-ordination is required because the movements involved from the start of the run-up to the recovery from the throw are complex and interlinked. To train to throw in competitions, I use mental rehearsal to visualise and map out all that is required in a successful throw.

9. Training is required to be specific to you performance needs, relevant to the activity and relevant to your fitness needs and ability.

10. Progressively overloading your body with higher training work rates will enable your body to adapt to the extra demands you have added. Progressive overload can be achieved through increasing the frequency, intensity and duration of the training programme.

11. Considerations of both these factors helps determine the intensity level that can be maintained for long periods of time without a build up of fatigue.

12. • It enables high intensity training to be undertaken while linking this training to periods of rest in a calculated way that will avoid fatigue occurring.
    • It has the capacity to be useful for both aerobic and anaerobic purposes.
    • Progressive overload can be carefully added to your training.

13. Plyometric training is based on powerful contractions (absorptions) by groups of muscles and on the concept that if muscles are pre-stretched before contraction then they can contract more flexibly. For example, players rebounding in basketball and spiking in volleyball might use plyometric training: here, standing tall and then bending down before a strong forceful jump is more effective than starting from an already low bent leg position.

14. There are three energy systems required in training. One (anaerobic) is for particularly short activities such as the 100 m sprint in athletics. A second is for particularly long (aerobic) activities such as the 10,000 m race in athletics. A third is designed to improve lactate tolerance. This is required for activities such as football where high intensity (anaerobic) sprints are required during times of high aerobic activity over a long period, for example the 90 minutes of a full football game.

15. Periodisation is the organisation of training into a carefully considered plan which involves different periods of training, each period having its own specific aims and purposes.

16. • It allows you to avoid fatigue prior to competition
    • It allows you time to complete your physical and mental preparations for competition

17. This is the first phase of training and includes pre-season training. General exercise training will be followed by more specific training which focuses on your particular requirements. This will cover your strengths and weaknesses, your role within activities and your existing fitness levels.

18. In a periodised training year, a period of overload is followed by a _taper_. This can last up to two weeks, during which time the training load is gradually _reduced_ before _competition_. This takes place to ensure that the fitness benefit of training is not reduced through the onset of fatigue. The degree of taper in a training programme will be affected by the demands of the _activity_. For example, in athletics, a sprinter's taper will be relatively _long_, whilst a long distance runner's taper might last only a few days.

ANSWERS TO COURSE ASSESSMENT REVISION QUESTIONS

Area 3: Skills and Techniques (see questions on pages 78-79)

1   A skilled performance would perform linked movements with maximum efficiency. As a result, you would expect to see qualities such as control, fluency, consistency, economy (effort) and effective decision-making through selecting correct options

2. The information processing approach to _learning_ involves considering the importance of _perception_ and decision-making. This approach centres on how well you learn to _read_ the information available and interpret correctly what to do in a _sequential_ order. There are four key stages involved. These are _input_, _decision-making_, _output_ and _feedback_.

3. It provides the basis for an evaluation of your performance by detailing the sequences through which practical skills are learned. As a result your plan of action for your strengths and weaknesses can be identified and monitored.

4. closed   5   6   1   2   3   4   open
    ⟵⟶

5. **Badminton**

    Most skills in badminton are open because they are carried out in an unpredictable way due to the actions of your opponent. However, there are some badminton skills that are essentially closed but also partially open. An example is the high serve. The intention here is to serve high to the back of the court. You control when to serve and can take care serve correctly. However, the actions of your opponent can still place some open skill demands on you. For example, his or her position on court can partially affect how you complete the serve. If he or she positions him- or herself towards the back of the court, you would need to consider the trajectory of the high serve or decide to play a low or flick serve instead.

6. • Mechanical analysis information might include judgements about how the body moves through consideration of centre of gravity, force/resistance, action/reaction, use of body levers and planes of movement.

    • Movement analysis information might include judgements about managing effort factors in performance and through the different phases of action such as preparation, action and recovery.

    • Consideration of quality might include judgements about different technical, physical, personal and special qualities.

7. It is important that practices have clear objectives and are progressive and specific to you. As a result, it is important to take into consideration your present stage of learning.

8. Example: Gymnastics   Basic technique: forward roll.
    Complex technique: forward roll to single leg standing.

    In a simple technique, the movements are relatively straightforward to learn. They tend to be used as the basis for the development of more refined and demanding techniques. For example, in the forward roll most performers can tumble forward in a tucked shape and regain a standing position. However, it is much more complex to forward roll to a single leg standing position because the balance and timing required involve much more fine motor control.

9. • At the planning stage, external feedback should be short and concise because the skill is new to you. You require advice which is straightforward to understand because you have yet to become familiar with the subroutines that make up the skill.

    • At the practice stage, external feedback can be provided less frequently. This is because it takes time for you to practice linking movements together. External feedback at this stage can become more detailed.

- At the automatic stage, much less external feedback is required. However, the fine detail of your performance might require attention. As a result, external feedback would be much more detailed.

10. Method of practice 'whole/part/whole'   Activity: Badminton

    Explanation:

    When performing the overhead clear, it became apparent that I was having difficulty transferring my weight during the action phase of the movement. I was able to devise specific practices that were useful in improving this part of the technique. This was achieved by having a partner 'feeding' me the shuttlecock so that I could groove the action of moving forward as I made contact with it.

11. Method of practice: gradual build-up

    Activity: Badminton – overhead backhand clear.

    Explanation

    I used gradual build-up for learning the overhead backhand clear. This is a very demanding clearing technique because it involves complex footwork and racquet control. Gradual build up was a useful practice method because I was able to increase the degree of difficulty in completing practices. For example, at the beginning I practised the movements on their own by shadowing a model performer. After this, I then gradually added to the demands of the practice by having to move in a fluent, controlled way prior to making my first attempts at playing the shot. I then practised the technique under additional time pressure by having to get into position quickly before returning an overhead backhand clear.

12. **Hockey**

    In a short corner in hockey, my role is to take the shot. The speed of the technique is such that other players need to selectively attend to the actions of the player taking the corner and the player stopping the ball prior to me taking the shot. It is not possible or desirable to look closely at your opponents' actions or to concentrate on my run up and footwork prior to playing the shot. It is necessary for me to focus on completing the technique and the small variables, such as the exact positioning of the ball when stopped as these can affect the outcome of the shot.

13. To succeed, it is best if you can set challenging but achievable targets as your goals. If you manage this then your level of internal motivation is likely to be high.

14. Feedback should be offered as soon as possible after the activity as possible. It is best if positive feedback is clear, precise and accurate.

15. **Squash**

    The two practices were aimed at improving my backhand boast. This shot is designed to be played from tight in your defensive corner to low at the front of the court on the opposite side. (See diagram 1.) The first practice involved me moving from the centre of the court to the corner and playing a shot from a deliberate feed that was to be returned after hitting the side wall only. (See diagram 2.) This practice suited my level of ability because I was at the practice stage of learning. I knew what the technique of the boast involved and was able to use effectively external feedback that was provided by my teacher.

    The second practice was more demanding. It involved playing a boast return to a serve that had hit both the side and back walls, and then playing out the point competitively. (See diagram 3.) This practice was well suited to my ability because I was now at the automatic stage of skill learning. At this level, I was able to watch the flight of the ball in more detail because I had worked out the footwork requirements in my earlier practices. By now, I was using mostly intrinsic feedback. This was because I was able to feel and judge how well I was playing the shot at the time. I knew whether it was an effective boast or not before my opponent played their next shot. This was because I could use the internal feedback about the shape of my swing and the contact I made with the ball.

ANSWERS TO COURSE ASSESSMENT REVISION QUESTIONS

Area 4: Structures, Strategies and Composition (see questions on page 93)

1. A structure involves different considerations such as role and relationships, formation and group and team principles. Such structures are applied though different strategies, for example through different formations that might be used in different games such as hockey. Composition considers the inventive nature of performance within different structures.

2. In football, we play a patient passing game until we suddenly quicken the pace and use speed to begin quick penetrating attacks. The change in tempo between slow, patient and fast, direct play is designed to surprise and place the defending team under pressure.

3. In dance, we deliberately focused our planning on ensuring that we covered all parts of the working area through changes in speed and direction. This would transfer well to our stage production when the audience would expect that all parts of the stage would be used.

4. In basketball, our guards tend to be fast and relatively small. However, the other forwards and centres tend to be taller and larger but less quick. Organising ourselves in this way makes sense because we were deliberately playing to our strengths though the roles and relationships we have adopted.

5. In volleyball defence, it is importance to defend the width of the net against opponents' spike attacks. This involves being able to block different attacks that might be played though the middle or from out wide on either side of the net. Depth is also important. My team needs to defend against spikes that get past the defenders at the net. In addition, the whole team needs to be fast and mobile to be able to move quickly to cover different possible lines of attack.

6. **Badminton**

   When playing a defensive court strategy, it is important that I play a wide variety of shots to my opponent. The idea is that these shots will be played away from the centre of the court to the far corners of the court. Playing this type of game will ensure that my shots make demands of my opponent in that he or she will need to return shots from wide and deep areas of the court. This strategy is deliberately meant to make demands on my opponent's court mobility.

7. **Football**

   When defending a corner, it is important that all players in the team can speak effectively to quickly arrange who is going to pick up and mark the attacking players in the other team.

8. **Dance**

   I used choreographic ideas to help add sensitivity and expression to my performance. I achieved this by interpreting my dance's stimulus in a way that added emotional feeling to my performance. For example, the mood in my performance was meant to show the contrast between happy and sad. I was able to use choreographic ideas that projected happiness and sadness in my performance. This was be achieved through contrasting fast, dynamic, outwardly expressive movements with slower, more restrained movements.

9. **Orienteering**

   When planning for competition, I took into account the scale of the map and the type of terrain. When the competition had begun and the control points had been entered, I made decisions about deliberately aiming off to get as quickly as possible to particular control points and about judging my pace to run at throughout the entire competition.